The

REASON

for

GOD

TIMOTHY KELLER

The
REASON
for
GOD

Conversations on Faith and Life

DISCUSSION GUIDE
SIX SESSIONS

ZONDERVAN®

ZONDERVAN.com/
AUTHORTRACKER
follow your favorite authors

**REDEEMER
CITY to CITY**

ZONDERVAN

The Reason for God Study Guide and DVD
Copyright © 2010 by Redeemer City to City and Redeemer Presbyterian Church

Requests for information should be addressed to:

Zondervan, *Grand Rapids, Michigan 49530*

ISBN 978-0-310-33047-9

Based on the *New York Times* bestselling book *The Reason for God: Belief in an Age of Skepticism.*

The Reason for God Study Guide and DVD were written and developed by David Bisgrove and Sam Shammas from material by Timothy Keller.

Interior design: Ben Fetterley

Printed in the United States of America

14 15 16 17 /DCI/ 26 25 24 23 22 21 20 19 18 17 16 15 14 13 12 11 10

CONTENTS

Welcome to *The Reason for God*. This discussion guide and accompanying DVD will help you and your group learn how to engage others in conversations on faith and life. Specifically it will help you think about six common objections to Christianity.

The guide and DVD are not about getting armed with arguments and answers so that they can be used as generic responses whenever anyone asks you about your faith. Rather you should start to become conversant with ways to sensitively, gently, humbly, and respectfully talk about the objections—whether in the context of a friendship or a group setting.

Each of the "discussions" that make up this guide focuses on an objection to Christianity. During the discussions you will:

- Read an opening thought and a summary of the objection
- Watch a DVD segment (about 20 minutes)
- Work through discussion questions about the DVD
- Read a final thought
- Pray

The DVD segments are of Dr. Timothy Keller filmed live and unscripted with a group of new friends sharing their beliefs and their thoughts about the objections. The group met over a six-week period and discussed each objection for about an hour and a half, and then each person was interviewed for about ten minutes. The DVD segments therefore represent only a portion of the actual discussions and interviews.

After each discussion question you will see notes in gray boxes. These are not intended as answers to be read aloud; rather they are notes to help guide and direct the discussion. Those leading the group should read these notes in advance and then ask members of the group to read sections, headings, or paragraphs aloud as necessary to keep the group focused and on topic.

This guide uses the New International Version (NIV) translation of the Bible.

Isn't the Bible a Myth?
Hasn't Science Disproved Christianity?

───────── OPENING THOUGHT ─────────

Read this thought aloud and then pray as you begin.

In 1993, archaeologists dug up the first outside-of-the-Bible reference to King David. Up until then, only the Bible talked about King David—there were no inscriptions, no archaeological digs, no other documents, nothing, that ever mentioned David. Does that mean that Christians could not believe there was a David before 1993? It does not work that way. Christians believe there was a King David because the Bible is the Word of God.

───────── THE OBJECTION ─────────

People say that there are many good things in the Bible, but you should not take it literally; you must not insist that it is entirely trustworthy and completely authoritative because some parts of the Bible are wrong, historically unreliable, and culturally regressive.

These verses are referred to at some point in the DVD.

Mark 15:20–21

And when they had mocked him [Jesus], they took off the purple robe and put his own clothes on him. Then they led him out to crucify him. A certain man from Cyrene, Simon, the father of Alexander and Rufus, was passing by on his way in from the country, and they forced him to carry the cross.

Romans 3:21–25

But now a righteousness from God, apart from law, has been made known, to which the Law and the Prophets testify. This righteousness from God comes through faith in Jesus Christ to all who believe. There is no difference, for all have sinned and fall short of the glory of God, and are justified freely by his grace through the redemption that came by Christ Jesus. God presented him as a sacrifice of atonement, through faith in his blood.

————————————— DVD NOTES —————————————

Watch the DVD of Discussion 1. Use the space below if you would like to take notes.

The notes in the gray boxes following the questions are not intended as answers to be read aloud. They are notes to help guide and direct the discussion.

1. Are people you know more troubled by the ethical aspects of the Bible or the historical? Why?

2. One of the participants on the DVD said,

   "The Bible is a wonderful text, it's complex, a lot of things going on, some people believe it to be the truth, I myself do not."

   Another said,

   "Jesus sacrificed himself—I'm not sure if there is evidence for that."

   Many people say the Gospel accounts of Jesus' life—his claims to be divine, the miracles he performed, his death on a cross, his rising from the dead— were written much later by church leaders who were trying to consolidate their power and build their movements, so they suppressed the evidence that the real Jesus was just a human teacher. How would you respond?

Following are three reasons why people can trust that what the Bible says about Jesus is historically reliable.

The New Testament accounts of Jesus were written too early to be legends.

Luke wrote his account of Jesus' life 30–40 years after the events, and he records the fact that many people who saw Jesus were still alive, and that his readers could therefore check his account with these eyewitnesses. In fact, Luke (in Luke 1:1–4) claims to be painstakingly preserving historical facts, "I myself have carefully investigated everything ... so that you may know the certainty of the things you have been taught." Luke's statement to Theophilus, the recipient of the text, shows that ancient authors knew the difference between an *"orderly account"* and spinning a tale.

This attitude toward history is not Luke's alone. In John 19:35 and 1 John 1:1–4, the writer claims to have been an eyewitness of the events of Jesus' life.

Paul, who wrote 15–20 years after the events of Jesus' life records, "He [the resurrected Jesus] appeared to more than five hundred of the brothers at the same time, most of whom are still living" (1 Corinthians 15:6). Paul could not have written that in a public document unless there actually were hundreds of living eyewitnesses who claimed to have seen Jesus. Paul could also confidently assert to government officials that the events of Jesus' life were public knowledge: "[These things were] not done in a corner," he said to King Agrippa (Acts 26:26). The people of Jerusalem had been there—they had been in the crowds that heard and watched Jesus. The New Testament documents could not say Jesus was crucified when thousands of people were still alive who knew whether he was or not. If there had not been a burial, if there had not been an empty tomb, if there had not been appearances after his death, and these public documents claimed there had been, Christianity would never have gotten off the ground. It would have been impossible for Christianity to have gained widespread support if its critical historical claims were bluntly contradicted by numerous witnesses who were still alive.

Moreover, there are references within the Gospel texts that demonstrate that the Gospel writers and readers had access to firsthand accounts of the events of Jesus' life. In Mark 15:21 the author can refer to "Alexander and Rufus" (the sons of the man who carried the cross for Jesus) in a way that shows they were well known to his readers. This was mentioned in the DVD where Dr. Keller said, "It is like footnotes today."

(cont.)

This shows that the Gospels were written by people in a position to get and report accurate historical information, and were written at a time when eyewitness memory about Jesus was still widely available as a "check" on any fantastic or fabricated claims.

The documents are too detailed in their form to be legends.

In Mark 4 there is a detail recorded which says that Jesus was asleep on a cushion in the stern of a boat. In John 21 it says that Peter was a hundred yards out in the water when he saw Jesus on the beach. He then jumped out of the boat and together they caught 153 fish. In John 8, as Jesus listened to the men who caught a woman in adultery, it says he doodled with his finger in the dust. The best explanation for why an ancient writer would mention the cushion, the 153 fish, and the doodling in the dust, when they are irrelevant to the narrative, is because the details had been retained in the eyewitnesses' memory.

The documents are too counterproductive in their content to be legends.

The argument goes that the Bible does not give an account of what actually happened; instead, it is what the church leaders wanted people to believe in order to consolidate their power and build their movement. However, if someone wanted to build a movement, would they have included in the account that their founder, Jesus, asked the Father for a way out: "If it is possible, may this cup be taken from me" (Matthew 26:39)? Would they attest that the original resurrection witnesses were women at a time when women's testimony was not admissible evidence in court? The leaders of the early church were the successors to the apostles, and yet on every page of the New Testament, the apostles look like fools or cowards. Why would a leader of the early church make up those accounts? The only possible explanation for their inclusion is that they actually happened. Otherwise, they are totally counterproductive.

3. Read the following objections aloud:

   A: "The Gospels are full of contradictions."

   B: "The Gospels can't be reliable accounts because they describe miracles."

   C: "Why should a person believe the Old Testament is true?"

   Divide into three groups and assign one of the objections above to each group. After five minutes regroup and share your thoughts on how you would respond to the objection.

   After coming up with your own thoughts and ideas, use the notes below to help you formulate a response to share with the group.

   A: "The Gospels are full of contradictions."

   Comparing the Gospel accounts reveals some apparent tensions and contradictions. But a long tradition of scholarly study has shown that most of these can be explained with reference to two principles.

   First, remember the Gospel writers were not simply reporters but also teachers. John says (in John 21:25) that it would be impossible to put together a complete account of all Jesus' teaching and acts. Each writer selected in accordance with his didactic, or teaching, goals.

   For example, many have said that John contradicts the other Gospels because he depicts Mary coming to the tomb alone on Easter Sunday. And yet, when Mary runs to the disciples, John reports her as saying, "They have taken the Lord out of the tomb, and we don't know where they have put him!" (John 20:2). Mary's use of the plural "we" shows that John knew full well that Mary had not gone to the tomb alone, and yet in the first part of his account he chooses to focus on her exclusively. Why? He wanted the interview of Jesus and Mary to be highlighted.

   (cont.)

Second, remember the selectivity of eyewitness memory. If, as they claim, the Gospel writers were drawing on eyewitness accounts (e.g., from the memory of Peter, John, Mark, or any of the women), each witness would have seen only part of the events.

Also, in some cases, a fact could be described different ways by eyewitnesses without being a contradiction. For example, John says Mary arrived at the tomb "while it was still dark" (John 20:1), but Matthew says it was "at dawn" (Matthew 28:1) and Mark says "just after sunrise" (Mark 16:2). At dawn, the degree of darkness or light is a matter of opinion, and so three different people, there at the same moment, might later describe that moment in all three ways.

B: "The Gospels can't be reliable accounts because they describe miracles."

Matthew Arnold, the 19th-century thinker, was candid about how he knew that miracles were impossible. He said effectively: "Miracles cannot happen. Therefore miracles have not happened."[1]

There is an intellectual inconsistency involved in objecting to the historicity of the Gospels because they contain miracles. To say "miracles cannot happen" is a philosophical assumption, not an empirical conclusion. If there is a God, miracles would have to be possible, even if you have never seen one. If a God exists who is capable of making the world, why should he be incapable of altering it? So to say miracles are impossible is to assume that there cannot possibly be a God, a thesis that is impossible to prove empirically, and therefore a philosophical assumption. This is arguing in a circle — "miracles cannot happen, *therefore* miracles have not happened."

C. S. Lewis wrote, "When the Old Testament says that Sennacherib's invasion was stopped by angels (2 Kings 19:35), and Herodotus says it was stopped by a lot of mice who came and ate up all the bowstrings of his army (Herodotus, Bk.II, Sect.141), an open-minded person will be on the side of the angels. Unless you start by begging the question [assuming miracles cannot happen], there is nothing intrinsically unlikely in the existence of angels or in the action ascribed to them. But mice just don't do these things."[2]

---

1. Paraphrase of the conclusion of Matthew Arnold in *God and The Bible* (New York: Macmillan, 1901).
2. C. S. Lewis, "Miracles," *God in the Dock* (Grand Rapids: Eerdmans, 1970), 27–28.

C: "Why should a person believe the Old Testament is true?"

There is a great deal of archaeological and historical support that validates much of the Old Testament. But that alone could not establish the divine inspiration of the Bible. Christians believe the divine inspiration of the Old Testament because Jesus taught and believed in its entire inspiration and trustworthiness (John 5:37–39, 46–47; 10:34–35; Matthew 5:17–19). Almost no one can doubt that Jesus, as a first-century Jew, believed in the authority of the Old Testament. If Jesus was who he said he was, then we must accept the entire Bible as God's Word.

In Matthew 5:18 Jesus says, "I tell you the truth, until heaven and earth disappear, not the smallest letter, not the least stroke of a pen, will by any means disappear from the Law [the Old Testament] until everything is accomplished." In John 10:35 he says, "Scripture cannot be broken." According to Jesus, even the smallest punctuation mark in the Old Testament is important—"the least stroke of a pen." That is the strongest statement about the Bible that can be made. On one occasion Jesus says to someone: "Are you not in error because you do not know the Scriptures or the power of God?" (Mark 12:24). Far from being full of errors, Jesus insists that the Bible is the way to keep from error.

And Jesus does not just say that every part of a letter of the Bible is true. He goes even further to say every part of the Bible *will* come true—he says it will all be accomplished. It is one thing to say the Bible is true. A phone book could be true. But Jesus goes beyond that—it will be accomplished. That means every prophecy will come true, every promise will be fulfilled. Every warning and every threat will be followed through on, and every single command will someday be obeyed because someday every nation will bow and every tongue confess that Jesus Christ is Lord. Scripture cannot be broken, it cannot be written off, not one part of it, because every part of it is the Word of God.

Interestingly in John 7:17 Jesus lays down this challenge to people who doubted his words: "If anyone chooses to do God's will, he will find out whether my teaching comes from God or whether I speak on my own." Jesus is saying that if you want to know in your own experience whether or not the Bible really is true, then put its teachings into practice.

4. **Read Matthew 28:16 – 17. One of the participants on the DVD said,**

"There are a lot of miracles that happen in the Bible, but … I've never seen a miracle along [the lines of] what happens in the New Testament."

How do people you know react to the idea of the miraculous? What does this passage teach about miracles?

Miracles are hard to believe in, and they should be. In Matthew 28 it says that when the apostles met the risen Jesus on a mountainside in Galilee, "they saw him, they worshiped him; but some doubted." That is a remarkable admission. Here is the author of an early Christian document saying that some of the founders of Christianity could not believe the miracle of the resurrection, even when they were looking straight at Jesus with their own eyes.

This passage shows several things. It is a warning not to think that only modern, scientific people struggle with the idea of the miraculous, while ancient, more primitive people did not. The apostles responded like any group of modern people would — some believed and some did not. It is also an encouragement to patience. All the apostles ended up as leaders in the church, but some had more trouble believing than others.

The most instructive thing about this text, however, is what it says about the purpose of biblical miracles. They lead not simply to cognitive belief, but to worship, awe, and wonder. Jesus' miracles in particular were never magic tricks, designed to impress and coerce. Instead, he used miraculous power to heal the sick, feed the hungry, and raise the dead. People tend to think of miracles as the suspension of the natural order, but Jesus meant them to be the restoration of the natural order. The Bible says that God did not originally make the world to be filled with disease, hunger, and death. Jesus' miracles are not just proofs that he has power, but wonderful foretastes of what he is going to do with that power. Jesus came and is coming again to redeem the world where it is wrong and heal the world where it is broken.

5. One of the participants said on the DVD,

"Evolution is very crucial for me—it being able to mesh into the Bible properly. Because I definitely believe in evolution. So, if the Bible says evolution does not exist, then I feel it loses credibility."

How would you respond to someone who felt that evolution makes biblical faith unacceptable?

A frequent objection to the credibility of Christianity is the seeming incompatibility between the "ancient" belief in a God who created the world and who, for example, performed miracles like the parting of the Red Sea, and the "modern" world of genomes, Darwin, and the scientific method. One area where this tension is strong is in the area of evolution—such that most people now think that if you believe in God you can't believe in evolution, and that if you believe in evolution you can't believe in God.

First, many believe that the account in the Bible of how the world was created completely contradicts the generally accepted idea that human origin is a function of evolutionary forces that can be explained in the natural world. It is important when discussing the Bible to ask that people take the time to honor the writers of the Bible by taking them seriously—which means, for example, asking the question "How does this author want to be understood?" One way to discern how an author wants to be read is to distinguish what genre the writer is using. Many people believe that the book of Genesis falls in the genre of "exalted prose narrative"—this means that the author was making truth claims about the world in which we live, but that he wrote it in such a way that it was not meant to be taken literally. For example, in Genesis 1 natural order means nothing (light appears before the sun is created), where in Genesis 2 natural order is followed (Genesis 2:5). So it seems clear that the author's primary intent was to show that "In the beginning *God created*." How he did it (i.e., in seven 24-hour days or over millions of years representing seven epochs) is not the point. Once this is understood, evolution, or any other scientific theory, is no longer contradictory to the Bible because the point of Genesis is that the omnipotent, personal God created and sustains all things.

(cont.)

Second, it is important to carefully define the terms when engaged in a discussion on this topic. So for example, if someone says something like, "I don't believe in God because I believe in evolution," one response might be, "What do you mean by evolution?" For most people today that word has come to mean an overarching way to describe who we are, how we got here, and where we are going. That is, everything from our morality to our aesthetics to our shared logic have been shaped by nondirected genetic mutation that helped our ancestors survive. This is a significant departure from understanding evolution as a biological process that explains how species have changed and adapted over the years. One is a worldview that is no less a faith position than Christianity; the other, a scientific hypothesis. One scholar summarizes it this way — "If 'evolution' is … elevated to the status of a worldview of the way things are, then there is direct conflict with biblical faith. But if 'evolution' remains at the level of scientific biological hypothesis, it would seem that there is little reason for conflict between the implications of Christian belief in the Creator and the scientific explorations of the way which — at the level of biology — God has gone about his creating processes."[3]

6. Was there anything in the way the DVD discussion was conducted in terms of tone, atmosphere, attitude, mannerisms, expressions, and so on, that you might find helpful to adopt, or not, when you run your own discussion about this objection?

Notice, for example, how much Dr. Keller speaks in the first 10 minutes of the discussion as opposed to the last 10 minutes. Is listening to people an important part of a group discussion?

3. David Atkinson, *The Message of Genesis 1–11*, The Bible Speaks Today Series, (Downers Grove, Ill.: InterVarsity Press, 1990), 31.

7. If you had to summarize the Bible from Genesis to Revelation in three minutes what would you say? Try it. You may want to divide the group into pairs to do this exercise.

Here, for example, is one way of doing this. You may want to choose someone to read this aloud to the group:

God's kingdom was present in the Garden of Eden. God lived there with his people and there was nothing but unclouded joy and fullness of life. But when his people decided to be their own masters, and reject God's authority, God's light and glory withdrew. And the big issue, the question of the ages, and the question on which the plot of the Bible hinges is—will he ever be back? Will his light and glory ever be on the earth again?

And then hundreds of years later, a man named Moses met God, and God said, "Build me a tabernacle and in the middle of the tabernacle, build a sanctuary, the holy of holies, and in there, my Shekinah glory, my kingdom presence will dwell." And when Moses built that tabernacle, God's glory came down and dwelled in the midst of the tabernacle, in the midst of the people. Yet, people could still not see God because his presence was dangerous to sinful human beings. And the people who lived around the tabernacle were constantly being rebellious, trying to be their own masters. So eventually, God removes his presence, and his glory and light are gone once again.

Then hundreds of years later, another man comes and wherever he went, glory and light went—diseases were healed, people were given new life. And on the night that he was killed, the veil that divided the people from the holy of holies was ripped in half. That means that because of Jesus' death, not only did he take the punishment for all sin, but people can go back into the presence of God—that his glory is present, his kingdom of power is now back. This power is in the people of God who know him, and that's why Jesus says, "I have given you the kingdom." And that kingdom power that was in the Garden of Eden, and then in the tabernacle, is now here. Eventually this kingdom will cover the entire earth, God's glory and light will take over the universe again, and the entire world will be a gigantic holy of holies—the New Jerusalem.

FINAL THOUGHT

Read this thought aloud.

Notice how 30 to 50 percent of each Gospel is given to the last week of Jesus' life. If you were telling the story of someone's life, why would you do that? The Gospel writers believed it was not the example and teaching of Jesus, but his saving work in history, his death and resurrection, that was the important and significant part. One of the participants said on the DVD, "Did Jesus come, die on a cross, or did he not? For me that is very important, that is the most important, because it holds all these ramifications with it. If he did do that, then that changes everything, as opposed to, if he didn't do that."

PRAYER

Spend time praying about the things you have learned in this study and how you might help people you know with this objection.

ADDITIONAL READING

The Reason for God, Timothy Keller (ch. 6, "Science Has Disproved Christianity," and ch. 7, "You Can't Take the Bible Literally")

Creation or Evolution: Do We Have to Choose?, Denis Alexander
Jesus and the Eyewitnesses, Richard Bauckham
The Historical Reliability of the Gospels, Craig Blomberg
The New Testament Documents: Are They Reliable?, F. F. Bruce
Science and Faith: Friends or Foes?, C. John Collins
Nothing But the Truth, Brian Edwards
Darwin on Trial, Phillip E. Johnson
Redeeming Science, Vern Poythress

How Can You Say There Is Only One Way to God?
What About Other Religions?

———————————— OPENING THOUGHT ————————————

Read this thought aloud and then pray as you begin.

If you put three swimmers on the coast of California and ask them to swim to Hawaii, the Olympic swimmer might swim 500 miles before she dies. The second swimmer might be a good swimmer, and swim 25 miles before he dies. And the last swimmer does not know how to swim very well and swims only one mile before he dies. So you might say that the Olympic swimmer is 500 times better as a swimmer than the third one. Who is more dead? Nobody can get to Hawaii on the basis of their own swimming ability. The Bible says we are supposed to love God with all our heart, soul, mind, and strength, and our neighbor as ourselves. Nobody gets there. The unique message of Christianity is that you "get there" not because of your own effort, your own good works, but because you put your trust in what Jesus did for you on the cross.

———————————— THE OBJECTION ————————————

People say that since there are so many ways to find God, Christianity is only one among many valid options. The other religions of the world have millions of adherents, producing much wisdom, character, and happiness, so Christians should not claim to have the best faith or the only true faith.

These verses are referred to at some point in the DVD.

Deuteronomy 29:29

The secret things belong to the LORD our God, but the things revealed belong to us and to our children forever, that we may follow all the words of this law.

Matthew 9:2–8

Some men brought to [Jesus] a paralytic, lying on a mat. When Jesus saw their faith, he said to the paralytic, "Take heart, son; your sins are forgiven." At this, some of the teachers of the law said to themselves, "This fellow is blaspheming!" Knowing their thoughts, Jesus said, "Why do you entertain evil thoughts in your hearts? Which is easier: to say, 'Your sins are forgiven,' or to say, 'Get up and walk'? But so that you may know that the Son of Man has authority on earth to forgive sins ..." Then he said to the paralytic, "Get up, take your mat and go home." And the man got up and went home. When the crowd saw this, they were filled with awe.

Matthew 25:31–33, 46

[Jesus answered], "When the Son of Man comes in his glory, and all the angels with him, he will sit on his throne in heavenly glory. All the nations will be gathered before him, and he will separate the people one from another as a shepherd separates the sheep from the goats. He will put the sheep on his right and the goats on his left.... Then they will go away to eternal punishment, but the righteous to eternal life."

John 8:58

"I tell you the truth," Jesus answered, "before Abraham was born, I am!"

Watch the DVD of Discussion 2. Use the space below if you would like to take notes.

The notes in the gray boxes following the questions are not intended as answers to be read aloud. They are notes to help guide and direct the discussion.

1. In *The Gospel in a Pluralist Society,* Lesslie Newbigin writes,

    In the past thirty years European peoples have become accustomed for the first time to the presence in their midst of large numbers of people of other faiths. It has not taken long for them to discover that many of these Hindus, Buddhists, Sikhs, and Muslims are devout and godly people.... Since the inter-religious issue is usually compounded by the inter-racial issue, and since we are aware of the racism which infects us so deeply, there are the strongest emotional reasons for regarding religious pluralism as something to be accepted and welcomed.... In a world threatened with nuclear war, a world facing a global ecological crisis, a world more and more closely bound together in its cultural and economic life, the paramount need is for unity, and an aggressive claim on the part of one of the world's religions to have the truth for all can only be regarded as treason against the human race.[4]

    Wilfred Cantwell Smith writes in his book *Religious Diversity,*

    Except at the cost of insensitivity or delinquency, it is morally not possible to go out into the world and say to devout, intelligent, fellow human beings: "... we believe that we know God and we are right; you believe that you know God, and you are totally wrong."[5]

    Discuss the implications of these statements. Why do you think people today are so insistent that all religions are equally valid?

4. Lesslie Newbigin, *The Gospel in a Pluralist Society* (Grand Rapids: Eerdmans, 1989), 25, 155–156.
5. Wilfred Cantwell Smith, *Religious Diversity* (San Francisco: Harper, 1976), 14.

It is important to understand the reasons why so many people are insistent that all religions are equally valid. The first one is a concern for unity. People conclude that we have to defang religion if we are ever to have peace in the world. They say something like this: "You may hold your particular beliefs, but you must not do so in such a way that delegitimizes the truths of other religions, faiths, and cultures."

The second and more personal issue is the experience of exclusion. Many people have felt coerced, excluded, and exploited by professing Christians.

There is a strongly held belief that religions in general erode peace on earth and lead to strife, conflict, and division. Christians need to admit the fact that this is true. In general, religion does not lead to peace on earth because it sets up a slippery slope in the heart—religion tells people they have the truth and this is the right way to believe and act, and that can make people feel superior to those who do not have the same beliefs and practices. That can lead to caricaturing others, separating from them, excluding them, thinking of them as less important people, and even justifying their marginalization, exclusion, or oppression.

2. Following are four objections that are raised regarding Christianity's claim to be the only way to God. Read them aloud.

   A: "All major religions are equally valid, produce much wisdom and happiness, and basically teach the same thing."

   B: "Lots of good and intelligent people differ with the Christian viewpoint, so it is arrogant to claim that Christian beliefs are the only true ones."

   C: "You can't hold people responsible for rejecting Jesus when they have never heard of him."

   D: "Nobody can know whose religion is true, so Christianity can't claim it is the only true way."

   Divide your group and assign the objections among them. Determine how you would handle that particular objection. After a few minutes share your answers with the group.

After coming up with your own thoughts and ideas use the notes below to help you formulate an answer to share with the group.

A: "All major religions are equally valid, produce much wisdom and happiness, and basically teach the same thing."

Christians need to agree wholeheartedly that much is true and virtuous about the other world religions. It is true that there is enormous consensus among religions on what constitutes ethical behavior. For example, it is true that (in quite different ways) every religion condemns greed and self-centeredness.

However, this objection is not as open-minded as it may first appear, because it does not listen to what the other religions are actually saying and papers over the differences between them. People who claim that the world's religions are different paths up the same mountain do not deny the fact that they differ in some particulars. To claim that all religions are basically the same is not to deny the differences between a Buddhist who believes in no god, a Jew who believes in one God, and a Hindu who believes in many gods. It is to deny that those differences matter. But this does not take seriously the beliefs and practices of the religion. This position claims to be promoting religious tolerance—but only after it requires every religion to deny its distinctives or to say the distinctives do not matter.

Most world religions have sharply different views of reality and consider those beliefs to be nonnegotiable; that their core beliefs are necessary for people to find salvation. Another irreconcilable difference between religions is over Jesus himself. Most religions insist Jesus could not be the unique Son of God, and Christianity says not only that he is but that it is necessary for salvation to believe this. In the DVD discussion Dr. Keller pointed out that Christianity differs from other religions in "how you are saved—that means the process by which you can know that your relationship with God is the way it should be."

So religious pluralism is not a tolerant attitude toward all religions, but a new religion itself that essentially asks every other faith to remake itself in the image of religious pluralism. In other words, it refuses to acknowledge the true diversity of world religions—often in the name of promoting diversity.

B: "Lots of good and intelligent people differ with the Christian viewpoint, so it is arrogant to claim that Christian beliefs are the only true ones."

Christians need to acknowledge and admit the terrible fact that the Christian church has never lacked for truly arrogant people. Truth claims will always attract arrogance and moral absolutes will always attract moralists.

Having said that, this illustration may help. Imagine that a research scientist claims she has discovered the cure to some fatal disease. Imagine that she immediately publishes articles and gives lectures about it that are arrogant in tone. It is true that her arrogance will move many people to try to prove her wrong. But does her *arrogance* prove that she is wrong about what she says? Would it be arrogant of a research scientist *per se* to declare, in *any* tone of voice, that she has found the cure that no one else has found? Then why would it necessarily be arrogant for any person to say that they had discovered a spiritual cure that no one else has found? They may be wrong about the claim, but it would not necessarily be arrogant.

However, the central premise behind the arrogance charge is one that religious pluralists have to apply to their own beliefs as well. Once religious pluralists become aware that others disagree with their belief about spiritual reality, then why is it not arrogant of them to continue to hold their beliefs? The person who says, "It is arrogant to persuade others to your religious position" is actually doing the very thing he is forbidding—at the moment he is forbidding it.

C: "You can't hold people responsible for rejecting Jesus when they have never heard of him."

When it comes to the question of people who have never heard about Jesus, Christians need to concede that they do not know everything God knows about this. But we are told clearly in the Bible that God is just and merciful; that it is necessary to believe in Jesus in order to come into a saving, personal relationship with God; and that God initiates that belief.

(cont.)

D: "Nobody can know whose religion is true, so Christianity can't claim it is the only true way."

The main problem with this objection is that it is a claim to massive religious knowledge itself—though it is hidden beneath a veneer of humility. It says, "No one can know about spiritual things," but that statement presumes an astonishing amount of spiritual knowledge. If you say, "I don't know which religion is true," that can be a statement of humility. If you say, "No one can know which religion is true," you are making a very dogmatic assertion and presuming the very "religious knowledge/certainty" you just doubted that anyone had. The only way you can be absolutely skeptical about religion and say nobody has all the truth, nobody has complete knowledge, is if you have complete knowledge.

3. Some people would argue that the religious pluralism objection is itself a religious belief, claiming to be more true than opposing beliefs, and as such is subject to all the criticisms it levels at traditional religions. Explain.

There is a flaw in the religious pluralism position that can be found in virtually any form of it (even the most sophisticated).

First, the religious pluralism view is a *belief*. It is not an empirically verifiable hypothesis. There is no way to prove it.

Second, the religious pluralism view is a *religious* belief. It is a belief about the nature of spiritual reality, and is quite a detailed description of that reality. Religious pluralism proponents assert that the ultimate is unknowable and so they do not believe (for example) that there is one God who accepts people because of the sacrifice of Jesus Christ. This is a series of beliefs about the nature of God and spiritual reality—it is a religious belief with explicit dogma.

Third, religious pluralism proponents want to persuade those opposing them. They believe that the world would be a better place if more people held the religious pluralism position on spiritual reality rather than traditional Christianity.

So, religious pluralism is a religious belief that claims to be a better or more accurate or preferable view of spiritual reality than other views. Of course the religious pluralism proponent may object: "I'm not saying anything specific about God—I'm only saying that we can't know for sure what he is or what he's like." But the Christian view of God is that God has revealed who he is so people *can* know him. To say "we can't know God for sure" is to assert that God has not revealed himself in this way. Religious pluralism objectors may deny that they are simply substituting one religious belief for others, but that is the case. Their position is unusually inconsistent. They say no one should claim that their understanding of religion is more right and superior to others, yet they maintain that their understanding is superior to others.

4. **One of the participants said on the DVD,**

   "I think problems arise whenever one group believes it has the exclusive domain on truth or the exclusive hold on truth. I think when you believe that you have the firm hold on truth it leads to extreme behaviors at the detriment of others who may not believe what you do—it leads to intolerance."

   People often say similar things when the topic of religion or truth claims comes up. The words *exclusive, divisive,* and *intolerant* are a common feature of these statements. How would you respond?

It is important to grant that often when this topic comes up the rhetoric does get heated and those who represent the Christian position are not always particularly respectful of those who disagree. And indeed there has been terrible intolerance by the church throughout history.

Having said that, just because people hold two contradictory positions does not necessarily mean the people are hostile—just that they hold two different views of ultimate reality. Everybody has a view of spiritual reality that is exclusive. Irreligion is exclusive, too. Everybody is basing their lives on truth claims that are fundamentals. Even people who say nobody has the truth are making a truth claim. So you cannot avoid truth claims. The question is, which truth claims lead to intolerance?

At the heart of the Christian's view of spiritual reality is a man who gave his life in sacrifice for people who did not believe in him, a man who died asking for forgiveness for the people who were killing him. Therefore, Christianity is an exclusive claim, but it is the most inclusive exclusive claim because it wants you to exclusively believe in this man who died for his enemies, and asks you to love and care for yours.

So, does the message that Jesus is the only way to God necessarily lead to intolerance? Christians can only become intolerant to the degree that they misunderstand the heart of the gospel—namely, the good news that Almighty God himself came to serve us and die for us, so we could be saved not because of our right beliefs and behavior, but by the gift of his unmerited grace. That message, rightly grasped, cannot lead to coercion or intolerance. The gospel has within it deep resources for humility and respect. It is up to Christians to prove this assertion with their lives.

As a side note, it is worth noticing that the pluralist approach does not in itself promote unity between faiths and cultures. For one thing, the idea that truth is relative and that every person has the right to construct his or her own religion is grounded in a highly individualistic way of thinking that many cultures do not share. Religious pluralism is therefore ethnocentric, the promotion of one particular cultural worldview as superior to others.

The fact is that anyone's main identity-factor—that which gives them a sense of significance—can be a basis for exclusion and oppression. Overt absolutists say, "What makes me special is that I have the truth"—and that leads to feeling superior to and to acting exclusively toward people who do not have your truth. Covert absolutists say, "What makes me special is that I know that there is no absolute truth and everyone is free to be who they choose to be." But this also leads to feeling superior to and to acting exclusively toward people who think that there is truth. But the gospel absolutist says, "I have the truth—but the truth I have is a suffering God, a lamb that was slain, the one who died for his enemies, the one who came not to be served but to serve and give his life a ransom for many."

5. **During the DVD discussion Dr. Keller asked the participants what they thought should be done about the divisiveness of religion. One participant responded,**

"Has there been a time on the earth where there wasn't religion, and what would it look like if religion were absent? Would it necessarily be a better place, would it be a less divisive place? I don't know."

Another said,

"All the negative aspects of religion are usually tied to extremists, people who take it more ... and more literally."

What would you have said in response to these statements? Is this how people you know would have responded? Discuss.

6. Stephen Carter (who was mentioned on the DVD) writes this,

> Efforts to craft a public square from which religious conversation is absent, no matter how thoughtfully worked out, will always, in the end, say to those of organized religion that they alone, unlike everyone else, must enter public dialogue only after leaving behind that part of themselves that they may consider the most vital.[6]

Is it possible to keep all religious views private — away from the public square?

There are three approaches that civic and cultural leaders around the world are using to address the divisiveness of religion. The first is hoping and expecting that religion will thin out and eventually go away. The second is forbidding or controlling it. The third thing people are trying to do about the divisiveness of religion is to urge that we privatize it. The strategy is that we can have peace on earth if all people who have religious beliefs privatize them; that is, never bring their religious beliefs into work, politics, or public discourse in general. We put our religious beliefs behind us and come together and just do what works.

Stephen Carter in the preceding quote says that this is an inequitable approach to civil life. Religion is a set of unprovable faith assumptions about the meaning of life, about who we are, and about what is really important for human beings to spend their lives doing. Some people call it a worldview or a meta-narrative. Even if you are not part of an organized religion, everybody has an implicit set of these religious faith assumptions. And so there is no way we can all get together, leave those behind, and say, "Let's just work pragmatically and find solutions that just work for everybody." One's view of what promotes human flourishing is rooted in these faith assumptions.

One of the participants on the DVD agreed with this point saying, "Everyone has a view of the world and it is impossible to separate that view of how things should be and what you believe politically."

---

6. Stephen L. Carter, *The Dissent of the Governed* (Cambridge, Mass.: Harvard University Press, 1990), 90.

7. **One of the participants asked,**

    "How do you pick your fundamental, your home? Is it the way you were raised? Is it your own research?"

    How do most people you know "pick" their religion or their home? How did you?

    It is helpful to note amid all the theological and philosophical points that could be made around this topic that this is also a personal question for people. It is about their own personal choices as well.

8. **Discuss how to handle the more personal side of this topic when you run your own discussion about this objection. Was there anything from the way the DVD discussion was conducted in terms of tone, atmosphere, attitude, mannerisms, expressions, and so on, that you might find helpful to adopt, or not?**

    Notice for example that Dr. Keller defined the words *saved* and *sin* when he used them. Sometimes a person's definition of a specific word, the Christian definition, and what people think is the Christian definition are three separate things.

9. God created us, we fell into sin, he has redeemed us—creation, fall, redemption. How could these three concepts give people a powerful basis to treat with respect and justice those with whom they deeply differ?

The doctrine of creation is that every human being has been made in the image of God. In Genesis 9 and James 3 God says we must treat every human being as sacred, regardless of what they do, regardless of what they have done in the past, and regardless of their behavior, because they are made in his image. Also, because they are made in God's image, all people are capable of words and deeds which are wise and beautiful. On the other hand, the doctrine of the fall (Genesis 3) says that we are all sinners, everyone, including Christians. And the biblical teaching on redemption means that sinners are saved by grace alone. Christianity is the one religion that says people are not saved by being better people, by being more disciplined, by praying more, by being more compassionate; people are saved by sheer unmerited grace.

If Christians understand the doctrines of creation, fall, and redemption, then they will expect a lot of non-Christians they meet to be moral, nice, self-controlled people—sometimes even nicer than some Christians. Christians also know that they are no different than anyone else—we "all have sinned and fall short of the glory of God" (Romans 3:23)—and so again they treat people with love and respect and a lack of superiority.

—————————————— FINAL THOUGHT ——————————————

Read this thought aloud.

You cannot actually be skeptical about one set of beliefs without a deep faith commitment to some other set of beliefs. You cannot avoid fundamentals and you cannot avoid truth claims. G. K. Chesterton said: "A bigot is not the one who thinks he's right. Every sane man or woman thinks they're right. The bigot is the one who cannot understand how the other person came to be wrong."[7]

—————————————— PRAYER ——————————————

Spend time praying about the things you have learned in this study and how you might help people you know with this objection.

—————————————— ADDITIONAL READING ——————————————

The Reason for God, Timothy Keller (ch. 1, "There Can't Be Just *One* True Religion")

The Dissent of the Governed, Stephen L. Carter
Answering Islam, Norman Geisler and Abdul Saleeb
The Abolition of Man, C. S. Lewis
Death of a Guru, Rabindranath R. Maharaj
Can Evangelicals Learn from World Religions?, Gerald R. McDermott
The Gospel in a Pluralist Society, Lesslie Newbigin
The Supremacy of Christ in a Post-Modern World, John Piper, et al
The Universe Next Door, James Sire
Christianity at the Religious Roundtable, Timothy Tennent

---

7. Quoted from G. K. Chesterton's essay "The Anarchist."

DISCUSSION 3

What Gives You the Right to Tell Me How to Live My Life? Why Are There So Many Rules?

──────────── OPENING THOUGHT ────────────

Read this thought aloud and then pray as you begin.

People say: "Every person or culture has to define right and wrong for themselves." But if you ask them, "Is there anyone in the world right now doing things you believe they should stop doing no matter what they personally believe about the correctness of their behavior?"—they would invariably say, "Yes, of course." Then the question arises, "Doesn't that mean that you *do* believe there is some kind of moral reality that is not defined by us, that must be abided by regardless of what a person feels or thinks?"

──────────── THE OBJECTION ────────────

People say that the Christian belief in an absolute, one-size-fits-all truth that is objectively true for everyone is subversive to our individual and communal freedom. Christianity is an enemy of authentic personhood, social cohesion, and even freedom.

These verses are referred to at some point in the DVD.

Luke 10:29-37

But he [an expert in the law] wanted to justify himself, so he asked Jesus, "And who is my neighbor?" In reply Jesus said: "A man was going down from Jerusalem to Jericho, when he fell into the hands of robbers. They stripped him of his clothes, beat him and went away, leaving him half dead. A priest happened to be going down the same road, and when he saw the man, he passed by on the other side. So too, a Levite, when he came to the place and saw him, passed by on the other side. But a Samaritan, as he traveled, came where the man was; and when he saw him, he took pity on him. He went to him and bandaged his wounds, pouring on oil and wine. Then he put the man on his own donkey, took him to an inn and took care of him. The next day he took out two silver coins and gave them to the innkeeper. 'Look after him,' he said, 'and when I return, I will reimburse you for any extra expense you may have.' Which of these three do you think was a neighbor to the man who fell into the hands of robbers?" The expert in the law replied, "The one who had mercy on him." Jesus told him, "Go and do likewise."

Colossians 1:21-23

Once you were alienated from God and were enemies in your minds because of your evil behavior. But now he has reconciled you by Christ's physical body through death to present you holy in his sight, without blemish and free from accusation—if you continue in your faith, established and firm, not moved from the hope held out in the gospel.

Ephesians 2:8-9

For it is by grace you have been saved, through faith—and this not from yourselves, it is the gift of God—not by works, so that no one can boast.

Matthew 19:4-6

"Haven't you read," [Jesus] replied, "that at the beginning the Creator 'made them male and female,' and said, 'For this reason a man will leave his father and mother and be united to his wife, and the two will become one flesh'? So they are no longer two, but one. Therefore what God has joined together, let man not separate."

Galatians 4:6

Because you are sons, God sent the Spirit of his Son into our hearts, the Spirit who calls out, *"Abba*, Father."

Watch the DVD of Discussion 3. Use the space below if you would like to take notes.

The notes in the gray boxes following the questions are not intended as answers to be read aloud. They are notes to help guide and direct the discussion.

1. **The French philosopher Foucault writes:**

   Truth is a thing of this world: it is produced only by virtue of multiple forms of constraint. And it induces regular effects of power.[8]

   Foucault is saying that truth claims are power plays. What is your reaction to this statement? Is it true?

   These supplementary questions may help: Does everyone make truth claims? How are truth claims power plays? Do truth claims in and of themselves lead to oppression?

   Foucault is saying that when you claim to have the truth, you are trying to get power and control over other people. If for example you made a truth claim such as "everyone should do justice," Foucault would question whether it was because you really love justice or because you want to start a revolution that would give you control.

   Jesus' condemnation of the Pharisees in Matthew 23 makes the same point as Foucault, when Jesus said in verses 2–4, "The teachers of the law and the Pharisees sit in Moses' seat. So you must obey them and do everything they tell you. But ... they do not practice what they preach. They tie up heavy loads and put them on men's shoulders, but they themselves are not willing to lift a finger to move them." In other words, the Pharisees' truth claims are ways of getting power; they are ways of justifying themselves and getting control over God and other people.

---

8. Michel Foucault, "Truth and Power" in *Power/Knowledge: Selected Interviews and Other Writings, 1972–1977* (New York: Pantheon, 1980), 131.

However, one cannot insist that all truth claims are power plays, that all truth claims destroy freedom. C. S. Lewis writes in *The Abolition of Man*: "But you cannot go on 'explaining away' for ever: you will find that you have explained explanation itself away. You cannot go on 'seeing through' things for ever. The whole point of seeing through something is to see something through it. It is good that the window should be transparent, because the street or garden beyond it is opaque. How if you saw through the garden too? It is no use trying to 'see through' first principles. If you see through everything, then everything is transparent. But a wholly transparent world is an invisible world. To 'see through' all things is the same as not to see."[9]

In other words, if you say all truth claims are power plays, then so is your statement. If you say that all truth claims about religion and God are just psychological projections to deal with your guilt and insecurity, then so is your statement. To say that no one should make truth claims because they are just power plays is itself a power play. Everybody makes truth claims. It is not making a truth claim that leads to oppression; it is the content of the truth claim and the way it is held that may or may not lead to oppression.

2. One of the participants on the DVD said, "I'm not exactly sure what freedom means." How do people you know define freedom? What is your definition of freedom? Divide into pairs to answer these questions and then share your answers with the group.

3. Some people argue that Christianity, with its rules and exclusive truth claims, is repressive to both individuals and communities because it divides communities rather than unites them and because it diminishes our humanity by robbing us of our freedom to determine our own path. How would you respond?

---

9. C. S. Lewis, "The Abolition of Man" in *The Essential C. S. Lewis* (New York: Touchstone, 1988), 458.

Concede frankly that this can be true, but only when the resources of Christianity are misapplied.

First, the Christian community is not alone in holding exclusive beliefs. By definition, every community has particular beliefs and practices that are held in common by its members. For example, if you are on the board of a club or in the leadership of some political party and then you change your views or change your position on some matter of importance to that club or party, you will be asked to leave. This is not intolerance or exclusivity—it is just that every community has goals or beliefs to which they hold people accountable. By definition, all communities are exclusive—but that does not make them intolerant.

Second, people think that what it means to be truly human is to be free to choose their own path, that what liberates humanity is to be free of restraints that dictate how we should live. But in many ways this idea (that freedom is the absence of restraints) misses the complexity of what freedom is. Remember the example from the DVD: you cannot just eat anything you want—you have to restrict your freedom (diet) to get the richer, deeper freedom of good health and longer life. Musicians restrict themselves now (practice) to be released later into the far richer and deeper freedom of being able to perform and express themselves.

Discipline and restraint liberate our full potential when they tap into our abilities and skills. The key therefore is not to avoid every kind of restriction and constraint—but to find the constraints that are liberating. If that is true when it comes to vocations, hobbies, sports—why wouldn't it also be true for the moral and spiritual realms? Freedom is not the absence of restrictions, it is the presence of the right restrictions. The laws laid down in the Bible are not there to limit us or oppress us, but are the blueprint on how to unleash our full human potential.

4. During the discussion Dr. Keller summarized one of the participant's points as,

"You, I think, are saying that it is not just Christians, and it is not even just religious people, but actually everybody ... is working off rules."

One of the participants responded,

"I've got young kids so we are busy imposing rules every day ... and the rules are empowering."

It seems that people do not have a problem with rules in general; but some would say that certain rules in the Bible, such as those about sex, restrict individual freedom. How would you respond?

God defines marriage and sex very carefully. Marriage is the union of one man with one woman, which must be publically acknowledged, permanently sealed, and physically consummated. The Bible envisions no other kind of marriage, nor sex in any other arena. Polygamy which infringes on the one man–one woman principle, or one-night stands which involve no public acknowledgment, or adultery, and so on, are all infringements of this design. Sex creates deep intimacy, oneness, trust, and communion between two people. Because sex is a God-invented way to say to another person, "I belong completely and exclusively and permanently to you"—it was not intended to be used outside the permanent, exclusive commitment of marriage.

People say that God wants to restrict the way we have sex. But don't we *all*? For example, very few people think it is acceptable for adults to have sex with young children. The issue is finding the right restrictions—the restrictions that will allow us to flourish (as the DVD put it, that are "in accord with your own design").

5. One of the participants on the DVD said,

"I believe there are some rules or stories that basically think that homosexuality is a sin. I think that might be a rule that in spirit was trying to be helpful, but played out in contemporary society can be very problematic."

How would you respond?

Acknowledge that often when this topic comes up the rhetoric gets heated—and those who represent the Christian position are not always respectful of those who disagree, nor do they have sound reasons for their position. Christians have no more or less of a right to tell other people how to live their lives than anyone else. But we all have ways we think the world should be; and we all have the right to try to contend for these views respectfully. The gospel—that we are saved only by sheer grace—should help Christians to do this without self-righteousness.

Homosexuality is not God's original design for sexuality—sex is designed for marriage between a man and a woman (see the notes on question 4). But that belief should have no impact on a church's or a Christian's desire to love and serve the needs and interests of all their neighbors, including gay people, people of other faiths, and so on.

Note that there is *not* widespread division over what the Bible says about homosexuality. All three branches of Christianity (Orthodox, Catholic, and Protestant) agree—and the vast majority of Bible scholars have agreed for centuries—on at least four things: one, that every mention of homosexual practice in the Bible says that it is wrong; two, that it is specifically prohibited in both the Old and New Testaments; three, that it did not just reflect the prejudices of the day—it cut against the views of ancient cultures; and four, that the whole arc of the Bible begins with a heterosexual marriage (Adam and Eve) and ends with the vision of one—the wedding feast in the book of Revelation.

6. **Aldous Huxley says,**

    The philosopher who finds no meaning in the world is not concerned exclusively with a problem in pure metaphysics. He is also concerned to prove that there is no valid reason why he personally should not do as he wants to do.[10]

    What are the implications of his line of reasoning?

    Huxley went on to say, "For myself ... the philosophy of meaninglessness was essentially an instrument for liberation ... political and ... sexual." Huxley was speaking very frankly. He is saying if there is a God, I'm not free. So if I'm going to be free, I'll have to decide there is no God. Indeed, if there is no God, then nothing has been created; there is no design. Nothing has an author and everything is meaningless. So he is effectively saying, it is all an accident, it means nothing—that is the price of absolute freedom.

7. Notice that at the start of the discussions people often give their opinions and state their issues one after the other and they may or may not be connected to what the previous person has said. Discuss how to handle this when you run your own discussion about this objection. Was there anything from the way the DVD discussion was conducted in terms of tone, atmosphere, attitude, mannerisms, expressions, and so on, that you might find helpful to adopt, or not?

    At one point, after one of the participants had given his opinion of the objection Dr. Keller summarized the participant's statement and then asked the rest of the group to comment on it. What did you think of this approach?

---

10. Aldous Huxley, *Ends and Means* (New York: Harper, 1937), 269–273.

8. One of the participants said,

    "I think ... rules ... are necessary for freedom. I think we can have an abyss
    of liberty where there is too much freedom, and then you become paralyzed
    because there are too many options."

    **Some people argue that the idea that real freedom is having no restraints or
    restrictions and being able to do whatever you want does not work. Explain.**

Here are some reasons why this idea of freedom does not work:

This view of freedom is naïve about the complexity of the human heart.

When people say, "I've got to be free to do what I really want"—they may be
naïve about how the human heart works. People have a lot of wants, and they
often contradict each other. For example: On the one hand people want to eat
anything they feel like. And on the other hand, they want to have good health.
What is freedom? They have to decide which of those wants is the liberating one
and which one will bring them into bondage. And right away they have already
started to alter their model. They have started to realize freedom can't just be
the lack of restrictions but finding the right restrictions.

This view of freedom is naïve about the complexity of motivation.

What is it that drives or motivates people? There are hundreds of choices we
have to make every day, and they are usually between good options. Why do we
choose the ones we do? Every person has an ultimate value, what is often in the
Bible called an idol. We all believe that if we could just attain that "one thing"
(e.g., money or status) we would find freedom. The trap is, unless that one thing
is God, the object of our pursuit ends up controlling us.

This view of freedom is naïve about the fabric of reality.

Reality is like a fabric. There is a pattern, a design to reality that must be
honored or the fabric tears or unravels. The classic illustration is a fish. A fish
has two things that make it perfect in water: gills that absorb oxygen from the
water, not the air; and fins that move through water, but not on land. The fish
must honor its design. It is designed for water, not for land. That is a restriction.

If it's in the wrong environment, if it's not able to honor the way it fits into the fabric of things, it dies. If it does honor its design, it is free to do all it was designed to do.

What are human beings made for? The clue is to look at how human love works. If you are selfish and you are not married, that is hard. If you are selfish and you are married, it is a disaster. John Stott put it this way, "True freedom is to be one's true self, but my true self is made for loving, and loving is self-giving. So in order to be myself, I have to deny myself and give myself. In order, then, to be free, I have to give up my freedom. In order, then, to live, I have to die to my self-centeredness. In order to find myself, I've got to lose it."[11]

Real freedom is not doing what we most want to do. Real freedom is knowing which of the things we most want to do is siding with what we were designed for. Real freedom is finding the right restrictions, and that is why Jesus says, "If you hold to my teaching ... you will know the truth, and the truth will set you free" (John 8:31 – 32); "Whoever finds his life will lose it, and whoever loses his life for my sake will find it" (Matthew 10:39); "Come to me, all you who are weary and burdened, and I will give you rest. Take my yoke upon you and learn from me, for I am gentle and humble in heart, and you will find rest for your souls. For my yoke is easy and my burden is light" (Matthew 11:28 – 30).

9. **Dr. Keller said on the DVD,**

"It is a little hard to understand how rules actually function inside the Christian faith. They actually don't operate the same way that rules operate in other philosophical systems or religious systems."

Explain.

Dr. Keller goes on to say, "Traditional religion says if I obey the rules, then God accepts me. Whereas Christianity says that because I believe in Christ who has done everything for me, he has died in my place, I am accepted—and therefore I obey the rules.... For Christians the rules are not at the center."

11. John Stott, unidentified sermon.

---------------------------------- FINAL THOUGHT ----------------------------------

Read this thought aloud.

One of the participants on the DVD said, "I don't have to experience some form of genocide to form an opinion about it. I have this overwhelmingly passionate feeling that any life should be protected if I can step in. Where does that come from? I don't know where that comes from."

---------------------------------- PRAYER ----------------------------------

Spend time praying about the things you have learned in this study and how you might help people you know with this objection.

---------------------------------- ADDITIONAL READING ----------------------------------

The Reason for God, Timothy Keller (ch. 3, "Christianity Is a Straitjacket")

Angry Conversations with God, Susan E. Isaacs
Mere Christianity, C. S. Lewis
Hope Has Its Reasons, Rebecca Pippert
Mere Morality, Lewis B. Smedes
Real Sex, Lauren Winner

Why Does God Allow Suffering?
Why Is There So Much Evil in the World?

———————————— OPENING THOUGHT ————————————

Read this thought aloud and then pray as you begin.

Albert Camus, the author and philosopher who was awarded the Nobel Prize for Literature, wrote, "The god-man [Jesus] suffers too, with patience. Evil and death can no longer be entirely imputed to him since he suffers and dies. The night on Golgotha is so important in the history of man only because, in its shadows, the divinity ostensibly abandoned its traditional privilege, and lived through to the end, despair included, the agony of death."[12]

———————————— THE OBJECTION ————————————

People say that the fact of appalling evil and suffering in the world is one of the main reasons they cannot believe in the traditional God of the Bible, because the God of the Bible is portrayed as a God who is both all powerful and all good. If that God exists, he would not create a world filled with pointless evil. Yet the world is filled with pointless evil, therefore the God of the Bible cannot exist.

---

12. Albert Camus, *Essais* (Paris: Gallimard, 1965), 444. Translated and quoted by Bruce Ward in "Prometheus or Cain? Albert Camus's Account of the Western Quest for Justice," *Faith and Philosophy* (April 1991), 213.

These verses are referred to at some point in the DVD.

Isaiah 14:24, 27

The LORD Almighty has sworn, / "Surely, as I have planned, so it will be, / and as I have purposed, so it will stand." ... / For the LORD Almighty has purposed, / and who can thwart him? / His hand is stretched out, / and who can turn it back?

Psalm 86:15

But you, O Lord, are a compassionate and gracious God, / slow to anger, abounding in love and faithfulness.

Hebrews 4:15

For we do not have a high priest who is unable to sympathize with our weaknesses, but we have one who has been tempted in every way, just as we are—yet was without sin.

John 3:16–17

For God so loved the world that he gave his one and only Son, that whoever believes in him shall not perish but have eternal life. For God did not send his Son into the world to condemn the world, but to save the world through him.

1 John 4:9

This is how God showed his love among us: He sent his one and only Son into the world that we might live through him.

Isaiah 53:5–6

But he [Jesus] was pierced for our transgressions, / he was crushed for our iniquities; / the punishment that brought us peace was upon him, / and by his wounds we are healed. / We all, like sheep, have gone astray, / each of us has turned to his own way; / and the LORD has laid on him / the iniquity of us all.

───────────────DVD NOTES───────────────

Watch the DVD of Discussion 4. Use the space below if you would like to take notes.

The notes in the gray boxes following the questions are not intended as answers to be read aloud. They are notes to help guide and direct the discussion.

1. Imagine this scenario: A friend comes to you upset because he or she has recently experienced some form of personal suffering (for example, the death of a loved one) and says, "I can't believe in a God who would allow this to happen to me—who would allow this evil and suffering." Order these possible responses from most to least helpful and explain why.

    A: Reassuringly and thoughtfully remind your friend that God always "works for the good of those who love him" (Romans 8:28).

    B: Gently and with compassion try to tell your friend about why God might allow their suffering.

    C: With compassion and love say things like, "I'm sure that somehow it's all going to work out for the best."

    D: Listen to your friend without saying much in response.

    E: Put an arm around your friend and kindly use phrases such as, "Remember, it will make you stronger."

Recognize that when talking to persons who are upset and say they can't believe in God because of the evil and suffering in the world, you cannot treat it primarily as a theoretical problem. They have clearly experienced some form of suffering, and so it is a personal issue. Even if a person is not upset, it may in fact still be the case.

The answer is always to listen and to respond with empathy and pastoral care. When people have just experienced a terrible tragedy it is not a good idea to try to comfort them by attempting to give them a reason for it. It probably is not helpful to say things like, "It will make you stronger," or "I'm sure that somehow it's all going to work out for the best." While these things may be true, they are not enough of a reason for the suffering.

Remember Bildad, Zophar, and Eliphaz. When Job was suffering terribly, these friends of his insisted there must be a reason for his suffering. In his case they believed he was not living in accordance to God's law. And at the very end of the book, God tells Job that he (God) is angry with these friends because they have not spoken of God what is right.

The response is to "mourn with those who mourn" (Romans 12:15).

One of the participants on the DVD said, "I grew up in a very Christian family.... If my parents see that I am struggling with something or there are challenges in my life, they explain it by saying, 'There is a greater purpose.' And there might be, but I find that to be a very limited explanation. It doesn't really comfort me, especially because what you want at that moment is alleviation. You don't want some grand explanation of why this is happening to you."

2. **David Hume in his famous discourses concerning natural religion writes:**

Epicurus' old questions are yet unanswered. Is God willing to prevent evil, but not able? Then he is impotent. Is he able, but not willing? Then he is malevolent. Is he both able and willing? Whence then is evil?[13]

How would you answer?

13. David Hume, *Dialogues Concerning Natural Religion*, ed. Richard Popkin (Indianapolis: Hackett, 1980), 63.

The idea is that, given the presence of evil—if God is good, he's not powerful; if he's powerful, he's not good. He couldn't be both powerful and good if evil is allowed to continue in the world, but if he's only one and not the other, then he's not the God of traditional Christianity.

But this objection to the existence of God hinges on a mistaken premise. It assumes that a good God would not allow evil to continue. But the reasoning underneath that premise goes like this:

1. *We* cannot think of any justifiable reason why God would allow suffering and evil to continue.

2. Therefore, God cannot have such a reason.

This logic does not hold. Why should there be no reason just because we cannot think of one?

Alvin Plantinga writes, "Suppose the fact is God has a reason for permitting a particular evil.... Is it even likely that we would wind up with plausible candidates for God's reason?... Given that he is omniscient and given our very substantial epistemic limitations, it isn't at all surprising that his reasons ... [might] escape us."[14] Plantinga also notes, "Why does God permit all this evil ...? Christians must concede that we don't know. That is, we don't know in any detail. On a quite general level, we may know that God permits evil because he can achieve a world he sees as better by permitting evil than by preventing it; and what God sees as better is, of course, better. But we cannot see why our world ... would be better ... or what, in any detail, is God's reason for permitting a given specific ... evil."[15]

In other words, if we have a God great enough to be angry at for not preventing evil and suffering, we must also have a God great enough to have a reason for allowing evil and suffering we cannot discern.

Moreover, if there is no God, people don't really have a good basis for being outraged at the existence of suffering. After all, nature is "red in tooth and claw." Death and destruction are perfectly natural. It is perfectly natural for the strong to eat the weak and "survival of the fittest" is a genetic principle. Someone can only object to injustice if they already believe in some kind of "supernatural"

---

14. Alvin Plantinga, *Warranted Christian Belief* (Oxford: Oxford University Press, 2000), 466–467.
15. Alvin Plantinga, "A Christian Life Partly Lived" in *Philosophers Who Believe*, ed. Kelly James Clark (Downers Grove, Ill.: InterVarsity Press, 1993), 70–71.

moral standard (some standard that comes from outside of nature and which judges some types of "natural" behavior as wrong). And where does such a supernatural standard come from if there is no God? So eliminating God does not eliminate the problem of evil and suffering.

3. **One of the participants on the DVD said,**

   "When the question is asked, 'Why does God allow suffering?' — my first thought is — why not? ... Suffering is life, that is a given, so there is no reason to question why it's there or even to extricate it from your life."

   Do people you know feel this way? Do you think this is a satisfactory answer to the problem of suffering? Discuss.

4. Over the years, people who try to defend the existence of God have come up with theodicies — good reasons why God allows evil. Read aloud the two most common theodicies below:

   A: *The Punishment Theodicy.* "Because humankind rebelled, the suffering of the world is the deserved punishment for sin."

   B: *The Free Will Theodicy.* "If God wanted people to freely choose the good, they would have to have been free to choose evil. The greater good of having true children (rather than robots) entails the risk of abuse of free will."

   Split into two groups and assign a theodicy to each group. What is helpful and what is problematic about the theodicy? Regroup after five minutes and share your answers.

After coming up with your own thoughts and ideas use the notes below to help you formulate an answer to share with the group.

A: The Punishment Theodicy

Helpful: Most objections to suffering presuppose that people deserve a comfortable life from God. But that premise has been smuggled in without support. How can we be so sure what kind of life we deserve from God? This theodicy helps expose the assumption that we are good people who deserve a good life by explaining sin and its consequences. Maybe the problem of evil is really—why does God allow so much happiness?

Problems: This theodicy leaves open the question of why God allows the distribution of the punishment to be so apparently random and oftentimes unfair. It also does not explain why God allowed human sin and thus evil in the first place.

B: The Free Will Theodicy

Helpful: Human freedom is an enormous good. As this theodicy points out, perhaps this freedom is worth the terrible evil that results from abuse of free will. A great deal of suffering in this world should not be blamed on God; it is the mean, cruel, inhuman choices people make that cause much of the evil. Even with natural disasters like landslides and floods, much of the suffering that results could be alleviated if we helped out more in the aftermath. Also things like greed, classism, racism, and oppression which often lead to poverty and social marginalization result in deaths that otherwise could have been avoided.

Problems: This theodicy still does not account directly for natural, nonhuman evil such as earthquakes. It also does not explain why God does not block the harm to others of our bad choices. We do not let a child run out in front of a speeding car to let him exercise his free will. Of course we would block major harm to the child. Why doesn't God do that? Is free will a good enough reason for all the evil? Free will has something to do with why there is suffering, but it does not completely explain it.

5. The Bible is filled with the cries of people — including many biblical authors — who are deeply perplexed and baffled by the magnitude and the unjust distribution of instances of evil and suffering. Can you recall some of these?

See for example: Judges 6:13; Job 23:2–9; Psalm 73:2–14; Ecclesiastes 7:15; Jeremiah 12:1–4; and Habakkuk 1:2–4.

6. The Bible is also filled with many verses that help Christians understand the general purposes for suffering. Can you recall some of these?

Christians suffer:

... for their own sake.

To learn who God is (Psalm 46; Daniel 4:24–37), to learn to trust God (2 Corinthians 1:8–9) and obey him (Psalm 119:67–72), to become more like Jesus (Romans 8:18–29), and to reach maturity of character (Romans 5:3–4; Hebrews 12:1–11).

... for the sake of others.

That God's people may have courage (Philippians 1:14) and power (2 Corinthians 4:7–12).

... for Christ's sake.

To identify with Christ (Galatians 2:20), and to share in his sufferings and glory (1 Peter 4:12–16; Philippians 1:29, 3:8–10; Romans 8:17–18; 2 Corinthians 4:17).

7. One of the participants on the DVD said,

"Things happen and we suffer and then later we gain understanding about what that suffering was."

Another said,

"I sweep it under the rug and just try and forget about it, just cross it out of my mind and pretend it never happened, and that's one way that I can usually deal with suffering."

What do you think of these responses? How do people you know usually deal with suffering?

Dr. Keller said on the DVD, "Two thing can happen when you suffer. One is you think, 'I'm being punished.' But the cross says, no, Jesus took your punishment.... The second question comes up, 'Well, maybe God doesn't care.' But the cross says God does care, he's lost a child out of his love for you."

8. Remembering the importance of discussing the personal nature of this topic, was there anything from the way the DVD discussion was conducted in terms of tone, atmosphere, attitude, mannerisms, expressions, and so on, that you might find helpful to adopt, or not, when you run your own discussion about this objection?

Notice that the discussion closes not with the philosophical, but with the personal—with the wounds of Jesus and how that speaks to the suffering of mankind. People's questions about Christianity are often not just theoretical, but have a personal aspect as well. That is easy to see with the topic of suffering, but personal issues may stand behind any intellectual objection. So, at one end of the spectrum people ask theoretical questions and may want simply to engage in a lively debate at an academic level. At the other end of the spectrum, there are questions that arise because people have been deeply hurt and are not looking for answers so much as needing someone to simply listen to their complaints with real respect.

Notice also that the participants are directing questions at one another.

9. **One of the participants of the DVD said,**

"How do I feel about a suffering God in Christianity? It actually made me think that it is a unique aspect of Christianity.... And I actually felt it might be a useful thing to help somebody get through a tragedy. It seemed like we need that. We need to feel that there are people, or there is a force, or some being that can empathize and go through these things with us. I think that that is something I realize in my own life and it seems like if Christianity can offer that, that might be a useful thing to think about."

Does the concept that God suffered help you deal with suffering? Give examples from your life or the lives of those you know.

Alvin Plantinga writes, "As the Christian sees things, God does not stand idly by, coolly observing the suffering of his creatures. He enters into and shares our suffering.... Some ... claim that God cannot suffer. I believe they are wrong. God's capacity for suffering, I believe, is proportional to his greatness; it exceeds our capacity for suffering in the same measure as his capacity for knowledge exceeds ours. We don't know why God permits evil; we do know, however, that he was prepared to accept suffering of which we can form no conception.... This doesn't answer the question, Why does God permit evil? But it helps the Christian trust God as his loving father.... His aims and goals may be beyond our ken ... but he himself is prepared to share much greater suffering in the pursuit of those ends. In this regard Christianity contains a resource for dealing with this existential problem of evil—a resource denied the other theistic religions."[16]

Though we cannot discern the reason that God might have for allowing evil, there is remarkable assurance that he does have one. He himself has suffered infinitely with us, for us, on the cross. This proves God is not indifferent to suffering, since he became involved, and that he must have some good reason that he will not simply end it.

The problem of evil and suffering is the strongest objection to the Christian faith. It is strong because it is an irreducible problem. It can never be removed by argument. However, evil and suffering creates an even greater problem for alternative views and positions. Atheists have no basis to be outraged at suffering and evil. Other religions have a God who does not suffer. Christianity is the only religion with a God that suffers. Only the Christian faith has a God who takes our misery and suffering so seriously that he is willing to get involved with it himself. God himself has come into our reality and experienced injustice, violence, and rejection. Confidence in the character of God—his love, his justice, and his wisdom—becomes possible only when people see what he did in coming himself to die on the cross in order to halt the greatest evil and suffering of all—separation from him.

The "theoretical" and "personal" answers converge here. What confirmation is there that God has some good reason for allowing suffering and evil to (temporarily) continue? The cross. God must hate evil, too, or he would not have done that. If he hates evil that much, he must have some good reason for letting history continue.

16. Plantinga, "A Christian Life Partly Lived," 71–71.

10. How does the Christian belief in the resurrection provide a resource for dealing with and understanding suffering?

Christianity says that when God comes back he is going to renew and cleanse this earth. Bodies, loved ones, homes will be restored, purified, and beautified. It will be a life in which God's people hug and eat and dance. Resurrection is the restoration of life. Jesus' resurrection means resurrection for all those who believe in him into this new heaven and new earth. It means that everything sad will come untrue, everything sad is going to be brought up into the future glory and is going to be made infinitely better for all the suffering and evil having once been true.

People can take comfort in the assurances that the eventual glory will make the suffering and evil experienced now infinitesimal. The DVD used this illustration: We can remember certain things happening to us that, as six-year-olds, we thought of as irreparable, tragic, emotional wounds that would never heal. Yet we got over them, eventually. We can therefore at least imagine the possibility of a glory and a bliss that goes on for a trillion years that could be so great, it would make anything we go through here look like a fairly dim memory.

Nevertheless, remember all this is a philosophical answer. If you are with a friend who is suffering, this is not something you should say. If you are actually in the midst of suffering right now, the answer is—there is no answer.

─────────────── FINAL THOUGHT ───────────────

Read this thought aloud.

Job repeatedly asked God to explain to him the reason for his suffering. And when God finally met with Job at the end of the book God never gave him an answer. And the fact is, that if at any point God had said to Job, "Let me tell you all the reasons why you're suffering" then Job would have said, "Oh, so that's it! I'm going to be famous, I'm going to inspire millions of people with my courage and nobility." Here's the irony—Job never would have become the great person that he became if he knew why he was suffering. And when we are in the middle of suffering, we should not try to imagine reasons that would justify it. That is really not the best thing for our heart.

─────────────── PRAYER ───────────────

Spend time praying about the things you have learned in this study and how you might help people you know with this objection.

─────────────── ADDITIONAL READING ───────────────

The Reason for God, Timothy Keller (ch. 2, "How Could a Good God Allow Suffering?")

Where Is God When Things Go Wrong?, John Blanchard
How Long, O Lord?, D. A. Carson
Making Sense Out of Suffering, Peter Kreeft
The Problem of Pain, C. S. Lewis
A Step Further, Joni Eareckson Tada
Lament for a Son, Nicholas Wolterstorff

Why Is the Church Responsible for So Much Injustice?
Why Are Christians Such Hypocrites?

――――――――――――― OPENING THOUGHT ―――――――――――――

Read this thought aloud and then pray as you begin.

In this peculiar way, Christianity is internally consistent—the church is full of sinners because in order to be a Christian a person has to admit that he or she is a sinner. In other words, it is not really a surprise that Christians sin, that there is an inconsistency between what they say and what they do, because the Bible explains again and again why people's hearts are drawn toward selfishness and pride and so on. The Bible says "this is how you should live if you believe this" but it also says "you can't, and you won't" and provides a solution to that problem in Jesus. Christianity, unlike other religions or self-help programs, acknowledges it cannot be followed perfectly.

――――――――――――― THE OBJECTION ―――――――――――――

People feel that they cannot identify with an institution such as the church or with Christian individuals when they see such an appalling record of injustice and hypocrisy.

These verses are referred to at some point in the DVD.

Matthew 6:1–6, 16–18

[Jesus said] "Be careful not to do your 'acts of righteousness' before men, to be seen by them. If you do, you will have no reward from your Father in heaven. So when you give to the needy, do not announce it with trumpets, as the hypocrites do in the synagogues and on the streets, to be honored by men. I tell you the truth, they have received their reward in full. But when you give to the needy, do not let your left hand know what your right hand is doing, so that your giving may be in secret. Then your Father, who sees what is done in secret, will reward you.

"And when you pray, do not be like the hypocrites, for they love to pray standing in the synagogues and on the street corners to be seen by men. I tell you the truth, they have received their reward in full. But when you pray, go into your room, close the door and pray to your Father, who is unseen. Then your Father, who sees what is done in secret, will reward you. . . .

"When you fast, do not look somber as the hypocrites do, for they disfigure their faces to show men they are fasting. I tell you the truth, they have received their reward in full. But when you fast, put oil on your head and wash your face, so that it will not be obvious to men that you are fasting, but only to your Father, who is unseen; and your Father, who sees what is done in secret, will reward you."

Ephesians 2:8–9

For it is by grace you have been saved, through faith—and this not from yourselves, it is the gift of God—not by works, so that no one can boast.

Watch the DVD of Discussion 5. Use the space below if you would like to take notes.

The notes in the gray boxes following the questions are not intended as answers to be read aloud. They are notes to help guide and direct the discussion.

1. One of the participants on the DVD said,

   "I think the objectionable Christians that I've seen ... I see them being judgmental, I see them being extremely self-righteous, and I see them holding people that they deem to be sinners to a different standard than they would themselves, and I find that to be extremely problematic."

   What do you think about this statement? Do you know people who feel this way?

2. How would you answer the charge that the church is judgmental and full of hypocrites?

> Acknowledge that this is sometimes the case. Sometimes this is because of a well-intentioned misunderstanding or misapplication of the Bible. Sometimes it is because Christians are sinners and are indeed judgmental and fail to live up to their standards. Sometimes it is through pure thoughtlessness. Even when Christians use phrases like, "Before I was a Christian I used to ...," they can come across as judgmental without meaning to come across in that manner.

Dr. Keller on the DVD defined a hypocrite as "an inconsistent person, a person that says one thing; does another, and knows that they are doing something wrong but puts up a front." Acknowledge that there are people like that in the church, just like there are everywhere else. But, then, there aren't many people whose lives really match their rhetoric. None of us is as kind or patient or generous as we know we should be, or as we want to be.

R. C. Sproul writes, "The Christian church is one of the few organizations in the world that requires a public acknowledgment of sin as a condition for membership. In one sense the church has fewer hypocrites than any institution because by definition the church is a haven for sinners. If the church claimed to be an organization of perfect people then her claim would be hypocritical. But no such claim is made by the church. There is no slander in the charge that the church is full of sinners. Such a statement would only compliment the church for fulfilling her divinely appointed task."[17]

3. **Dr. Keller said on the DVD,**

   "Why wouldn't a church be a place where you would find inconsistent, broken people, who don't always get it right?"

   Can you give examples of people from the Bible who are thought of as great or important figures, but who were also broken or flawed in some way? Divide into pairs to do this and then share your answers with the group.

The examples are numerous. Two obvious ones from the Old and New Testaments: King David, who was Israel's greatest king and greatest poet, was also an adulterer and murderer. Peter, who was one of Jesus' closest disciples and a leader of the early church, lied to protect himself and betrayed Jesus.

---

17. R. C. Sproul, *Reason to Believe* (Grand Rapids: Zondervan, 1982), 78–79.

4. In his book *God Is Not Great*, Christopher Hitchens addresses a hypothetical question he was asked on a panel with radio host Dennis Prager: If he were alone in an unfamiliar city at night, and a group of strangers began to approach him, would he feel safer, or less safe, knowing that these men had just come from a prayer meeting? Hitchens answers,

> "Just to stay within the letter 'B', I have actually had that experience in Belfast, Beirut, Bombay, Belgrade, Bethlehem, and Baghdad. In each case ... I would feel immediately threatened if I thought that the group of men approaching me in the dusk were coming from a religious observance."[18]

Hitchens then gives detailed descriptions of the tense social and political situations within these cities, which he attributes to religion. Many people believe that religions like Christianity inevitably lead to violence and oppression. How do you respond?

Start by stating that this is a fair point—violence done in the name of Christianity (or any religion or philosophy) is a terrible reality and must be both addressed and redressed. Acknowledge also that any religion can take transcendent ideas like cosmic good and evil, and combine them with feeling like their beliefs are superior to everyone else's—and that mixture can turn explosive.

However, one problem with the statement that religion leads to violence is that it is too simplistic. The communist regimes of the 20th century (atheistic by design) perpetrated horrific acts of violence and injustice in the name of the state. These societies were rational and secular—yet they inflicted violence against their own people without the influence of religion. It appears that there

---

18. Christopher Hitchens, *God Is Not Great: How Religion Poisons Everything* (Toronto: McClelland and Stewart, 2007), 18.

is something deep in human nature that leads us to make some idea or value transcendent or absolute (whether an explicitly religious one or not) in order to either claim some superior moral ground or as an excuse to oppress and do violence to others. There are sad and inexcusable examples in which professing Christians have failed to resist this impulse, but the universality of violence means we cannot pin the problem on religion. The problem is within us.

5. One of the participants on the DVD said,

"I thought the point was really compelling—it actually struck me—trying to put yourself in the shoes of the person rather than interpret their actions through your own lens."

Do people you know generally behave like this? Why or why not? Why might it be important to do this?

6. What do you tend to do when you read a text in the Bible that you do not immediately understand and whose meaning offends and/or upsets you?

7. What advice would you give persons who read a text in the Bible that they do not immediately understand and whose meaning offends and/or upsets them?

Four things to do when you get to a text of the Bible that offends or upsets you.

Consider the possibility that it does not teach what you think it teaches.

In Luke 24:13–32 the Emmaus disciples are upset because they think the Scripture teaches something it does not. Jesus tells them they do not understand.

Be patient with the text. Many of the things people find offensive can be cleared up with a decent commentary that puts the issue into historical context. The text may not be teaching what you think it is.

Consider the possibility that you are misunderstanding what the Bible teaches because of your own cultural blinders or the possibility that you may be offended by certain biblical texts because of an unexamined assumption of the superiority of your own cultural moment.

The Emmaus disciples misunderstood the prophecies about the Messiah because as Jews they were thinking of the redemption of Israel and not the redemption of the world. It is very easy to read a passage through cultural blinders and therefore misunderstand what the text actually teaches.

Moreover, people may say a passage is regressive and offensive because it is a problem for their culture, but other cultures may think the same passage is perfectly acceptable. For example, in some cultures, what the Bible says about sex is a problem, but there are no issues with what it says about forgiveness. In other cultures, they like what the Bible says about sex, but what the Bible says about forgiveness is considered ridiculous. Why should one set of cultural sensibilities trump everybody else's?

If the Bible really is the revelation of God and not the product of any one culture, why wouldn't it offend some cultural sensibilities at some point? Consider that the problem with some texts might be based on an unexamined belief in the superiority of one historical moment over all others.

Distinguish between the major themes and message of the Bible and its less primary teachings.

If people say, "I can't accept what the Bible says about gender roles, or politics," ask them to keep in mind that Christians themselves differ over what some texts mean. However, Christians all agree that Jesus rose from the dead on the third day. People do not need to worry about gender roles until they have decided what they think about the central teachings of the faith.

They may appeal, "But I can't accept the Bible if what it says about gender is outmoded." Respond to that with this question—"Are you saying that because you don't like what the Bible says about gender roles that Jesus couldn't have been raised from the dead? If Jesus is the Son of God, then we have to take his teaching seriously. If he is not who he says he is, why should we care what the Bible says about anything else?"

Remember that all of Scripture is about Jesus.

Jesus tells the Emmaus disciples that they misunderstood the Scripture— Christ had to suffer these things. Why did they misunderstand? The key is Luke 24:27—"And beginning with Moses and all the Prophets, he explained to them what was said in all the Scriptures concerning himself." Jesus is saying, "Everything in the Bible is about me."

If you think the Bible is all about you—what you must do and how you must live—then you do not need Jesus. All you need are the rules. There are only two ways to read the Bible: you can read the Bible as if it is all about you and what you must do to please God and be a good person, or you can read the Bible as if it is all about Jesus and what he has done for you.

8. Was there anything from the way the DVD discussion was conducted in terms of tone, atmosphere, attitude, mannerisms, expressions, and so on, that you might find helpful to adopt, or not, when you run your own discussion about this objection?

Notice for example how Dr. Keller dealt with criticism of the church and of Christians.

9. On the DVD Dr. Keller quotes Martin Luther who said, "All of life is repentance."[19] Explain.

Christianity is often equated with obeying the rules; being a morally superior person; having an unshakeable certainty of being right. Actually, most religions operate on this principle: "If I live as I ought, I will be accepted by God." But Christianity has a completely different operating principle—"If I am accepted by God as a gift through what Christ has done, then I will try to live as I ought." Christians are people who understand that they will always fail to live as they should, and that therefore they need forgiveness and grace. The prerequisite to becoming a Christian is admitting that you have this problem and that you need God's help. So continual repentance should be a mark of a Christian's life. Only people who rely on religious morality for their relationship to God instead of grace can maintain a sense of superiority toward those who do not believe and live as they do. Only people who do not routinely repent can be thoroughgoing hypocrites.

19. Martin Luther, "Disputation of Doctor Martin Luther on the Power and Efficacy of Indulgences" (1517), Thesis 1: "Our Lord and Master Jesus Christ ... willed that the whole life of believers should be repentance."

10. Dr. Keller said on the DVD,

"In the Old Testament and especially in the New Testament with Jesus, there are internal self-critiques by the believing community on ... religious hypocrisy or in the New Testament 'pharisaism.'"

What is the difference between "pharisaism" (or moralism) and the gospel?

Dr. Keller continued, "The difference between a Pharisee in the New Testament and a Christ-follower is not that the Pharisee and the Christian aren't both trying to obey God, they actually are ... but [the Pharisee] is doing it not only self-righteously and feeling superior to other people but when they do wrong they won't admit it and so there is not this theme of humble repentance."

When Jesus preached what has become known as the Sermon on the Mount he gave a strong rebuke of religious hypocrisy or moralism. He criticized those who prayed, who gave their money to the poor, who obeyed the rules. Jesus was clearly not against those things, but he was pointing out that often people do those "religious" things in order to feel superior to others. Jesus understood that perhaps the chief danger of the kind of religious moralism in which a community felt they had earned God's favor was that it would lead them to feeling that they deserved deference and respect from all other communities.

Instead, Jesus taught that the "last will be first" (Matthew 19:30); that you find your life by giving it away (Mark 8:35); that "it is more blessed to give than to receive" (Acts 20:35); that no one is good enough to earn God's favor (Luke 18:18–30).

Jesus himself lived that out by sacrificing his life so that his followers could be reconciled to God. Christians follow someone who sacrificed everything to redeem and renew the world. At the heart of the Christian faith is a man who died a victim of injustice and who called for the forgiveness of his enemies. This is why the paradoxical symbol at the center of Christianity is not a great throne embossed with gold but a wooden cross stained with blood. It is weird that people walk around with crosses as jewelry—it is like having little electric chairs as earrings. But it is because at the center of Christianity is a God who surrendered his power so that others could live.

FINAL THOUGHT

Read this thought aloud.

The effect of the Christian message is that it changes your identity. Your identity becomes defined by what God has done for you in Jesus; in what God thinks of you in Jesus. If that identity is not beginning to show itself in your attitude toward other races and classes, toward the poor and oppressed, toward people who differ from you in their opinions or beliefs, you may say that you have faith but your faith is dead.

PRAYER

Spend time praying about the things you have learned in this study and how you might help people you know with this objection.

ADDITIONAL READING

The Reason for God, Timothy Keller (ch. 4, "The Church Is Responsible for So Much Injustice")

The Transforming Vision, Brian Walsh, J. R. Middleton
Let Justice Roll Down, John Perkins
Church History in Plain Language, Bruce L. Shelley
Creation Regained, Albert Wolters
Until Justice and Peace Embrace, Nicholas Wolterstorff

How Can God Be Full of Love and Wrath at the Same Time? How Can God Send Good People to Hell?

Read this thought aloud and then pray as you begin.

"Because of your stubbornness and your unrepentant heart, you are storing up wrath against yourself for the day of God's wrath, when his righteous judgment will be revealed. God 'will give to each person according to what he has done.' To those who by persistence in doing good seek glory, honor and immortality, he will give eternal life. But for those who are self-seeking and who reject the truth and follow evil, there will be wrath and anger" (Romans 2:5–8).

"There will be a time of distress such as has not happened from the beginning of nations until then. But at that time your people—everyone whose name is found written in the book—will be delivered. Multitudes who sleep in the dust of the earth will awake: some to everlasting life, others to shame and everlasting contempt" (Daniel 12:1–2).

THE OBJECTION

People can accept the idea of a loving and forgiving God—but cannot accept a God who would knowingly send people to hell. Hell seems incompatible with the idea of a loving God.

These verses are referred to at some point in the DVD.

2 Thessalonians 1:6–10

God is just: He will pay back trouble to those who trouble you and give relief to you who are troubled, and to us as well. This will happen when the Lord Jesus is revealed from heaven in blazing fire with his powerful angels. He will punish those who do not know God and do not obey the gospel of our Lord Jesus. They will be punished with everlasting destruction and shut out from the presence of the Lord and from the majesty of his power on the day he comes to be glorified in his holy people and to be marveled at among all those who have believed.

Revelation 20:15

If anyone's name was not found written in the book of life, he was thrown into the lake of fire.

Revelation 21:21–22

The great street of the city was of pure gold, like transparent glass. I did not see a temple in the city, because the Lord God Almighty and the Lamb are its temple.

Romans 1:18, 21, 28–29

The wrath of God is being revealed from heaven against all the godlessness and wickedness of men who suppress the truth by their wickedness.... For although they knew God, they neither glorified him as God nor gave thanks to him.... Furthermore, since they did not think it worthwhile to retain the knowledge of God, he gave them over to a depraved mind, to do what ought not to be done. They have become filled with every kind of wickedness, evil, greed and depravity.

Revelation 21:1–5

Then I saw a new heaven and a new earth, for the first heaven and the first earth had passed away.... And I heard a loud voice from the throne saying, "Now the dwelling of God is with men, and he will live with them. They will be his people, and God himself will be with them and be their God. He will wipe every tear from their eyes. There will be no more death or mourning or crying or pain, for the old order of things has passed away." He who was seated on the throne said, "I am making everything new!"

Watch the DVD of Discussion 6. Use the space below if you would like to take notes.

The notes in the gray boxes following the questions are not intended as answers to be read aloud. They are notes to help guide and direct the discussion.

1. One of the participants on the DVD said,

    "I am at ease with taking the burdens of my own sins, I don't need somebody else to relieve that for me. I don't need to think about an afterlife, because I'm scared to live this life. There is a famous quote that says, 'People who live a full life aren't scared to die.' And for me, I'm living a full life and I'm not scared to take the brunt of my sins, I'm not scared to do what I need to do to live this life."

    Do people you know feel like this? What is your reaction to this statement?

2. How would you help someone to reconcile the fact that the Bible seems to be making two contradictory statements: that God is a God of love and a God of wrath?

> Thinking about our own relationships shows that these two aspects—love and wrath—are not incompatible. There is actually a correlation between how deeply we love someone and the extent to which we might get angry with them. For example, if you had a brother or a close friend who was battling with some self-destructive behavior or addiction which was ruining his life, you would not just sit by indifferently—you'd be angry at him, you'd confront him, you would not be afraid to offend him by passing judgment on his behavior. The greater

80

our love for someone, the greater our potential for anger at what is destructive in their lives.

One of the participants on the DVD said, "I as a parent ... I'm often full of love and wrath. It's not contradictory—being full of love and full of wrath is not at all contradictory—it happens all the time, sometimes at the same time."

A. W. Pink, in his book on the attributes of God, defines God's wrath this way: "The wrath of God is His eternal detestation of all unrighteousness. It is the displeasure and indignation of Divine equity against evil. It is the holiness of God stirred into activity against sin.... God is angry against sin because it is a rebelling against His authority, a wrong done to His inviolable sovereignty.... Not that God's anger is a malignant and malicious retaliation, inflicting injury for the sake of it, or in return for injury received. No; while God will vindicate His dominion as Governor of the universe, He will not be vindictive."[20]

Remember on the DVD Dr. Keller defined wrath as "settled opposition and hatred of that which is destroying what we love."

In God's case, God's wrath flows from his love for his creation. He is angry at injustice, greed, self-centeredness, and evil because they are destructive. And God will not tolerate anything or anyone responsible for destroying the creation and the people that he loves.

3. **One of the participants on the DVD said,**

"Hell and heaven exist now.... In any moment when your actions are negative or the influence is coming from, 'I want to do what I want to do,' instead of from the larger picture, you are in a sort of hell, because your ego has taken over. Whereas you are in heaven more when you are really compassionate and acting with others."

Do people you know feel this way? Is this true?

20. A. W. Pink, *The Attributes of God* (Swengel, Pa.: Reiner, 1968), 76.

4. The Bible has many things to say about heaven and hell. So does the popular press. It is worth distinguishing between the two. Each member of the group should find one verse or passage in the Bible about heaven and one about hell. Share these with the entire group. Then, summarize what you have learned from the verses you found.

Jesus was the most loving man who ever lived and yet he spoke more about hell than anyone else. He experienced it himself—on the cross. Jesus was separated from his Father—he knows what hell is like and he does not want anyone to be there.

The Bible describes hell as:

- "punished with everlasting destruction and shut out from the presence of the Lord and from the majesty of his power"—2 Thessalonians 1:9
- "where the fire never goes out," "their worm does not die, and the fire is not quenched"—Mark 9:43, 48
- "darkness"—Matthew 8:12; 22:13; 25:30; 2 Peter 2:17; Jude v. 13
- "fiery lake of burning sulphur," "lake of fire"—Revelation 19:20; 21:8; 20:10, 14–15
- "beaten with many blows"—Luke 12:47
- "weeping and gnashing of teeth"—Matthew 8:12; 13:42; 22:13; 24:51; 25:30

Hell is a terrible fate—no sacrifice is too great to avoid it. As Jesus says, "If your hand causes you to sin, cut it off. It is better for you to enter life maimed than with two hands to go into hell, where the fire never goes out" (Mark 9:43).

Hell is eternal, but it is not inevitable. As Peter wrote in one of his letters, "But do not forget this one thing, dear friends: With the Lord a day is like a thousand years, and a thousand years are like a day. The Lord is not slow in keeping his promise, as some understand slowness. He is patient with you, not wanting anyone to perish, but everyone to come to repentance. But the day of the Lord will come like a thief. The heavens will disappear with a roar; the elements will be destroyed by fire, and the earth and everything in it will be laid bare. Since everything will be destroyed in this way, what kind of people ought you to be? You ought to live holy and godly lives as you look forward to the day of God and speed its coming. That day will bring about the destruction of the heavens by fire, and the elements will melt in the heat. But in keeping with his promise we are looking forward to a new heaven and a new earth, the home of righteousness" (2 Peter 3:8–13).

Isaiah 60 and Revelation 21 are descriptions of eternity.

First Corinthians 15:35–52 describes the resurrection body: "But someone may ask, 'How are the dead raised? With what kind of body will they come?'... The body that is sown is perishable, it is raised imperishable; it is sown in dishonor, it is raised in glory; it is sown in weakness, it is raised in power; it is sown a natural body, it is raised a spiritual body.... Listen, I tell you a mystery: We will not all sleep, but we will all be changed—in a flash, in the twinkling of an eye, at the last trumpet. For the trumpet will sound, the dead will be raised imperishable, and we will be changed."

5. Some Christians make the argument that nobody goes to hell unless they want to. Is this true? Explain.

Hell and heaven essentially are our freely chosen identities going on forever. In other words, Christianity believes that people have a soul that lives forever, and therefore, a process that begins in our soul now can go on forever.

For example, take self-centeredness. As we know, the more self-centered people get, the more miserable and the more in denial they become. That is to say, they blame everybody else for their problems. And that is part of what self-centeredness is—you are wise in your own eyes, you can't take the blame for anything, nothing is ever your fault. Hell is a self-centered ego going on for a billion years.

God, according to Romans 1, lets people have what they most want—and hell is simply serving yourself, going on forever. Hell is God giving you the life you want, on into eternity.

Therefore, in a sense, nobody ever goes to hell in the Christian understanding unless they want to. People go to heaven because they love God and want to submit to him. People go to hell because they want to be away from God, because they do not want somebody telling them how to live their life. They want to live their own lives their way. Hell is separation from God. And, therefore, nobody goes to hell except people who want to go there.

In some ways, the fairest understanding of the afterlife is the Christian one, which says God gives you what you want. If you want to live with God forever, that's heaven, and you get it. If you want to be your own person, your own savior, your own lord, that's hell, and you get that—and you stay wanting it; you do not suddenly change your mind.

In Ezekiel 18:30 God says, "I will judge you, each one according to his ways." But the verse goes on with God pleading with his people: "Repent! Turn away from all your offenses.... Why will you die?... I take no pleasure in the death of anyone.... Repent and live!" (Ezekiel 18:30–32).

God's justice is active, not passive, and when we violate it God will judge. But what these verses also show is that God wants people to repent and turn to him—that he does not want anyone to perish.

6. One of the participants on the DVD said,

"I would like to think that I'm acceptable to God if I have good intentions, if I have a will to be good, if I have a will to love, if I try hard to be a better person."

You often hear people say things like, "Surely all good, decent people can find God and go to heaven." How would you respond?

It sounds open-minded to say: I believe that any good person can find God, not just Christians. But the premise behind that statement is that good people find God and bad people do not. There are two problems with the premise. First, it holds out no hope for bad people, and lots of us know deep down that we have not lived up to even our own moral standards. Second, it misunderstands Christians' beliefs. It assumes that Christians believe that they are going to heaven because they are good, and that is not true at all.

Christians believe that no one goes to heaven or hell by being compliant with Christian ethics—by being moral and good, or not. The essence of sin is loving anything more than the true God, and by essentially being our own "god"—that is, trusting ultimately in our own wisdom and ability. Even if you believe in God and are very good and moral, you may be doing it as a way to earn your own salvation, so that God will be obligated to bless and help you, and take you to heaven. The fact is, all of us—religious and irreligious, moral and immoral—are trying to control our own lives rather than rely on God. Everyone is doing this and we will not "find God" until we admit this spiritual condition and seek pardon and change through Jesus. Our eternal destiny is dependent *not* on being good but on our response to the grace of God and to Christ's death on a cross in our place, and on our willingness to admit that we are cut off from God because of the pride and self-centeredness of our hearts.

7. Dr. Keller asked the participants,

"Can you imagine why it would be good to believe in judgment day?"

Can you remember some of their answers to this? Add some of your own responses.

After sharing some ideas you may want to rewatch this section of the DVD.

8. Was there anything from the way the DVD discussion was conducted in terms of tone, atmosphere, attitude, mannerisms, expressions, and so on, that you might find helpful to adopt, or not, when you run your own discussion about this objection?

Notice for example how in this discussion (and in the previous ones) the responses keep presenting Jesus as the primary differentiator and apologetic for Christianity.

9. When people get rid of the idea of judgment and hell to make God more loving, they end up making him less so. Do you think this is true or not? Discuss.

David Martyn Lloyd-Jones uses the following illustration: Imagine a friend tells you that he has paid a bill for you. How should you respond? You have no idea until you know the size of the bill. Until you know how much he paid, you do not know whether to shake his hand or fall down and kiss his feet.

Unless you believe in hell, you will never know how much Jesus loves you and how much he values you.

On the cross Jesus cried, "My God, my God, why have you forsaken me?" (Matthew 27:46). To lose the love of a friend hurts but to lose the love of a spouse hurts more. The deeper the relationship, the more devastating and agonizing is the loss of it. On the cross, when Jesus lost the eternal love of the Father, he experienced an agony, a disintegration, an isolation greater than we would experience in an eternity in hell. He took the isolation and disintegration that we deserve upon himself. Unless you believe in hell and see what Jesus took for you, you will never know how much he loves you. Jesus Christ was the judge of the earth who came not to bring judgment but to bear judgment and go to hell for us. It is possible to *honor* a God that loves everybody. But if we want to be transformed, if we want to sense God's love around us, we have to believe in a God who loves everybody and yet also believe in a God who will judge everybody.

So, ironically, when people get rid of the idea of judgment and hell to make God more loving, they make him less loving.

10. Dr. Keller ended the DVD talking about the resurrection. If someone asked you why you believe that Jesus rose from the dead and why that belief is helpful to you, what would you say?

In his 800-page book *The Resurrection of the Son of God*, historian N. T. Wright says that there is no historically possible alternate explanation for the birth of the Christian church than the bodily resurrection of Jesus. There is a tremendous amount of evidence.

The Greeks, the Romans, the Jews in Jesus' day all had different worldviews — but the bodily resurrection of Jesus would have been as absolutely inconceivable to all of them as it is for us, just for different reasons. What kind of objective, overwhelming evidence would it take to smash their worldview and bring them to absolute certainty that Jesus was bodily raised from the dead? People today say that it would have to be incredible evidence for them to change their own worldview. Whatever it would take for us, something just as overwhelming must have happened to them.

We know what it was for them because the Gospel writers tell us: at least eleven times Jesus actually appeared, and hundreds of witnesses believed in the risen Christ because they saw him, heard him, and touched him, and thousands more believed because they believed the eyewitness testimony of their friends and neighbors. It overwhelmed them, and it changed their world. We have the same eyewitness testimony available to us.

How can you be totally sure when you look at all the horrible stuff that has happened in your life and out in the world that someday God is going to make it all right? How can you not just hope so, but be absolutely sure that in spite of your own failures, God loves you and will never let you go? How can you know that when you face death it is not the end? Only if you know that Jesus rose from the dead and therefore so will you.

Read this thought aloud.

"For [God] has set a day when he will judge the world with justice by the man he has appointed. He has given proof of this to all men by raising [Jesus] from the dead" (Acts 17:31).

"Just as man is destined to die once, and after that to face judgment, so Christ was sacrificed once to take away the sins of many people; and he will appear a second time, not to bear sin, but to bring salvation to those who are waiting for him" (Hebrews 9:27–28).

──────────── PRAYER ────────────

Spend time praying about the things you have learned in this study and how you might help people you know with this objection.

──────────── ADDITIONAL READING ────────────

The Reason for God, Timothy Keller (ch. 5, "How Can a Loving God Send People to Hell?")

The Difficult Doctrine of the Love of God, D. A. Carson
Original Sin: A Cultural History, Alan Jacobs
The Great Divorce, C. S. Lewis
Exclusion and Embrace, Miroslav Volf
The God I Don't Understand, Christopher Wright

Now that you have completed these "discussions" you may want to start your own group to help people you know think about the six objections.

There are resources available to help you do this at *www.thereasonforgod.com*. These include a series of questions to help you lead a group conversation on the objections you have looked at in this guide.

There are several ways to run the discussion group:

- You could simply pose the questions that form the titles of each "discussion" and see where the conversation leads.
- You could ask people to read the corresponding chapters from *The Reason for God* book and meet to discuss the chapters—like a book group.
- You could show the DVD, or clips from the DVD, and use these as a discussion starter. The website gives you further questions to help lead the group if you decide on this approach.

"Always be prepared to give an answer to everyone who asks you to give the reason for the hope that you have. But do this with gentleness and respect" (1 Peter 3:15).

ACKNOWLEDGMENTS

The Reason for God Discussion Guide was written and developed from material by Timothy Keller by David Bisgrove and Sam Shammas.

The project would not have been possible without the expertise and constant good humor of Scott Kauffmann and Juliet Vedral.

We are deeply grateful to: Andrew Hunt and his team for the masterful direction and production of the DVD; Kathy Keller and David McCormick for their counsel and support; Greg Clouse, Robin Phillips, T. J. Rathbun, John Raymond, and the rest of the Zondervan team for their guidance and expertise in getting it published.

This discussion guide is dedicated to Brian, Eddie, Eunice, James, John, Liz, Menon, and Sarah, who so generously gave their time and shared their lives on film.

gospelⁱⁿlife is an intensive eight-session course on the gospel and how it is lived out in all of life—first in your heart, then in your community, and then out into the world.

Session 1 opens the course with the theme of the city: your home now, the world that is. Session 8 closes the course with the theme of the eternal city: your heavenly home, the world that is to come. In between, you will look at how the gospel changes your heart (sessions 2 and 3), changes your community (sessions 4 and 5), and changes how you live in the world (sessions 6 and 7).

1 **City** The World That Is

2 **Heart** Three Ways To Live

3 **Idolatry** The Sin Beneath The Sin

4 **Community** The Context For Change

5 **Witness** An Alternate City

6 **Work** Cultivating The Garden

7 **Justice** A People For Others

8 **Eternity** The World That Is To Come

The study guide contains Bible studies, discussion questions on the DVD, and home studies. The home studies consist of a series of readings, quotations, exercises, questions, and projects to help delve deeper into the topic of each session. The guide also includes an extensive section of notes to help leaders prepare.

Gospel in Life Study Guide: 978-0-310-32891-9
Gospel in Life DVD: 978-0-310-39901-8

AVAILABLE ONLINE OR AT YOUR FAVORITE BOOKSTORE!

ZONDERVAN®
.com

www.redeemercitytocity.com
www.gospelinlife.com

REDEEMER
CITY to CITY

TWO SONS, ONE WHO KEPT THE RULES RELIGIOUSLY AND ONE WHO BROKE THEM ALL. ONE FATHER WHO LOVED BOTH LOST SONS BEYOND ANYTHING THEY COULD IMAGINE.

The Prodigal God curriculum kit contains everything that your church needs to experience a six-week preaching and small group campaign.

In this compelling film and study, pastor and *New York Times* bestselling author Timothy Keller opens your eyes to the powerful message of Jesus' best-known—and least understood—parable: The Parable of the Prodigal Son.

Dr. Keller helps you and your small group or church glean insights from each of the characters in Jesus' parable; the irreligious younger son, the moralistic elder son, and the father who lavishes love on both.

SESSION TITLES:

1. The Parable
2. The People Around Jesus
3. The Two Lost Sons
4. The Elder Brother
5. The True Elder Brother
6. The Feast of the Father

Session one contains the full 38-minute film. Each of the other five sessions will feature a short (2-3 minute) recap segment from the full length film to set up the small group discussion.

THE KIT CONTAINS ONE OF EACH OF THE FOLLOWING:
The Prodigal God DVD, *The Prodigal God* Discussion Guide, *The Prodigal God* hardcover book, and "Getting Started Guide." *Mixed Media Set 978-0-310-32075-3*

ALSO AVAILABLE:
Discussion Guide *(purchase one for each group member) 978-0-310-32536-9*

DVD *(purchase one for each group) 978-0-310-32535-2*

Hardcover book *(available in case lots of 24 only) 978-0-310-32697-7*

PICK UP A COPY AT YOUR FAVORITE BOOKSTORE!

ZONDERVAN®
.com

www.theprodigalgod.com

REDEEMER CITY to CITY

Share Your Thoughts

With the Author: Your comments will be forwarded to the author when you send them to *zauthor@zondervan.com*.

With Zondervan: Submit your review of this book by writing to *zreview@zondervan.com*.

Free Online Resources at
www.zondervan.com

Zondervan AuthorTracker: Be notified whenever your favorite authors publish new books, go on tour, or post an update about what's happening in their lives at www.zondervan.com/authortracker.

Daily Bible Verses and Devotions: Enrich your life with daily Bible verses or devotions that help you start every morning focused on God. Visit www.zondervan.com/newsletters.

Free Email Publications: Sign up for newsletters on Christian living, academic resources, church ministry, fiction, children's resources, and more. Visit www.zondervan.com/newsletters.

Zondervan Bible Search: Find and compare Bible passages in a variety of translations at www.zondervanbiblesearch.com.

Other Benefits: Register yourself to receive online benefits like coupons and special offers, or to participate in research.

ZONDERVAN®

ZONDERVAN.com/
AUTHOR**TRACKER**
follow your favorite authors